EVER~~...~~ **RE REMARK,**
EVERY ~~...~~
CA~~...~~
SELF-D~~...~~

Get out of my way!	Which way is yours?
Go to hell!	You mean this isn't it?
You think you're so clever!	Okay. Tell me when to start.
You should think before you speak!	Why should I have an unfair advantage?
...and hundreds more!	

NOW YOU CAN TURN
EVEN THE MOST OUTRAGEOUS SLINGS
AND ARROWS
INTO SHARP-EDGED BOOMERANGS!

WHY DIDN'T I SAY THAT?

THE ART OF VERBAL SELF-DEFENSE

by Donald Carroll

PUBLISHED BY POCKET BOOKS NEW YORK

POCKET BOOKS, a Simon & Schuster division of
GULF & WESTERN CORPORATION
1230 Avenue of the Americas, New York, N.Y. 10020

Published by arrangement with Franklin Watts
Library of Congress Catalog Card Number: 79-22265

ISBN: 0-671-44582-0

First Pocket Books printing February, 1982

10 9 8 7 6 5 4 3 2 1

POCKET and colophon are trademarks of Simon & Schuster.

Printed in the U.S.A.

FOR MY PARENTS
*who did their best to teach me
not to talk back, and failed*

Contents

Putting Words in Your Mouth

Does this situation sound familiar?

You are being questioned, or accused, or insulted, or nagged, or teased, or just plain bored by somebody—and yet you can't call a halt to the conversation because you don't know what to say. Later on, you play back the conversation in your mind, and suddenly you think of the perfect retort, the one that would have bailed you out of your predicament if only you had thought of it at the time. Frustrated, you ask yourself: "Why didn't I say that?"

Unfortunately, you have probably never taken the trouble to answer that question properly. The chances are that whenever you have suffered an attack of paralysis of the tongue, you have shrugged it off as just another example of your shyness, or inarticulateness, or tendency to panic under pressure, or . . . , but it doesn't matter how you diagnose the problem, because such a diagnosis completely misses the point anyway. Worse, it perpetuates the problem, and ensures that it will come back to haunt you again and again.

Psychologists have now begun telling us what political strategists have always told us: People do not treat us the way they do because of the way they are, but because of the way we are. Without us as accom-

11

plices, they could never have gotten into a position of power over us in the first place. As Machiavelli wrote in *The Prince:* "One who deceives will always find those who allow themselves to be deceived."

The same goes for people who bully, browbeat, bore, or otherwise behave in ways that are tiresome. They wouldn't do it if they didn't know they could get away with it. Lenin summed it up most graphically in his famous dictum: "Advance with bayonet. If you encounter mush, proceed. If you encounter steel, withdraw." That says it all—from the *aggressor's* point of view, that is. What it doesn't say is how those people who are inclined to turn into conversational mush can steel themselves against the verbal thrusts of others.

Words. That's the answer. Words, and more words.

For anyone who belongs to what might be called the awkwardly silent majority—those of you who find yourselves repeatedly at a loss to know what to say to people who are determined to be provocative or antagonistic—the solution to your problem is, very simply, to talk your way out of it. And keep talking.

I am well aware that there is nothing novel or revolutionary about this advice. Indeed, by now, there is little that is novel about *any* published advice, given the fact that within the past decade or so a whole psychological arms industry has grown up to supply the defense needs of those who consider themselves bashful, vulnerable, put-upon. Almost daily, or so it seems, there comes off the autotherapy assembly lines new and improved ways of pulling your own strings, making contact, standing up and talking back, saying "No" without feeling guilty, watching out for number one, winning through intimidation, achieving Power! and

Success! (and, who knows, if you're lucky, maybe even Happiness!).

Fine. Excellent weapons systems, all of them. The trouble is not that they don't work, but that they come without ammunition. It's like sending someone out to fight a duel with an unloaded dueling pistol: However splendid the gun, and however sharp your aim, without bullets your chances of winning the duel, or indeed of surviving it, must be reckoned as slim.

In short, before you can even begin to master the art of verbal self-defense, *you have to have the words*.

There is no particular merit in asserting yourself just for the sake of being self-assertive. As a matter of fact, it can be exceedingly risky. There is even less merit—and more risk—in continually talking back just to show that you can't be pushed around. Anyone who has children knows how easy it is to find someone willing to talk back to you. And any child who makes it a practice to talk back can tell you the likely outcome of such behavior.

This is not to say that a defensive posture isn't effective in discouraging aspiring bullies. But it has two serious drawbacks. One is that it tends to make you a person whose company is not greatly sought after. The second and more serious drawback is that, while it might work to repel certain types of threats, it leaves you doubly vulnerable to others.

Look at the example of the skunk. No creature on earth has a more effective and recognizable posture of defiance: That hoisted tail is enough to send the most fearsome grizzly crashing through the woods in the opposite direction. Yet, for this very reason, the skunk's reputation is such that he is forced to lead a very restricted social life, and on those occasions when he encounters a threat that remains unimpressed by his defiant posture—like, for instance, a Buick traveling at eighty miles an hour—the result of his defiance is apt to be a lingering stink in the air and a little fur on the highway.

The lesson is the same for those who find themselves menaced verbally or conversationally: Before you can deal effectively with the situation, you must first identify the exact nature of the menace. The person who is spoiling for a fight and the person who is unintentionally spoiling your fun represent two entirely different species of pest. Thus, they require different types (as well as different doses) of pesticide.

Hearing Is Believing

Before you can deal effectively with conversational challenges—whether subtle or bombastic, devious or direct—you must cultivate a rare skill: *the ability to hear what is actually being said to you*. This is not as simple as it sounds.

Actually, it *is* as simple as it sounds. It's just that we *make* it complicated because we have been conditioned to hear what is meant rather than what is said.

Consider the basic, straightforward question: "Do you know what time it is?" If you are like most people, you have seldom, if ever, given the equally basic, straightforward answer that question demands. This is not because you were trying to be evasive or unhelpful, but because you were so busy paying attention to the tone, inflection, gestures that accompanied the question—in other words, to what was left *unsaid*—that you didn't hear what was actually said.

For example, suppose that you are late for a dinner party, and while you are getting dressed your spouse comes into the room and asks, in a voice reeking with impatience: "Do you know what time it is?" The question you hear is: "What's taking you so long?" So you respond with something like: "Look, I can't help it if I had to work late. I'm hurrying as fast as I can."

Or suppose it's later that same evening and your spouse, obviously weary, stifles a yawn and asks: "Do you know what time it is?" The message that comes through is: "I'm awfully tired. Can't we go home?" Your reply: "Don't worry, we'll leave in a few minutes."

Finally, suppose you're at work and you pass someone holding his watch to his ear and looking perplexed. He stops you and asks: "Do you know what time it is?" You immediately take in the circumstances of the question so that it becomes: "I think my watch has stopped. What time do *you* have?" And you answer: "I have a quarter past ten."

Same question, three different answers. In the first instance, hearing the exasperation behind the question, you responded to the exasperation rather than to the question. In the second instance you heard desperation, so you replied reassuringly. In the third, you received an obvious desire for information, so you answered informatively. In none of these instances, however, did you answer the question you were asked.

There are, strictly speaking, only two possible correct answers to the question, "Do you know what time it is?"

"Yes." "No." Everything else is embroidery.

Now, there's nothing wrong with embroidering your conversations—on the contrary, in most cases it is altogether appropriate—*as long as you know what you are doing*. It's when you are unaware that you are

answering questions that were never asked, or reply-
ing to statements that were never made, that you get
into trouble.

Thomas Hobbes, the seventeenth-century English
philosopher, once wrote that there are only three ways
by which one person can become subject to another:
by conquest, by birth, and by voluntary offer. Rough
translation: If you live in a free society, and if you
don't live with your parents, then the only way that
someone can get the better of you is if you ask for it.

The reason that so many people *do* ask for it is
that they automatically assume that there's more to
any phrase or sentence than meets the ear. And of
course they're right. Even the simplest declarative
statement carries a subliminal message which you ignore at your peril. But that doesn't mean you should
address yourself to the hidden meaning of something
that is said to you—the shadow message, as it were—
and disregard the surface meaning. If you do, you will
play right into the hands of your conversational adver-
saries. In effect, you will have become a co-
conspirator against yourself.

To see how this happens, imagine a dialogue between two people as constructed like one of those children's drawings which are made by connecting a lot of
numbered dots. One party to the dialogue puts in the
dots, the other draws the lines that connect them. The
first person is clearly in command here, because he has
numbered the dots in such a way as to lead the second
person into creating precisely the sort of image that the
first one had in mind. In this analogy, the numbers
correspond to the "hidden meaning" in sentences:
They aren't really hidden at all. In fact, they are tan-
talizingly visible, so that the other person will be en-
couraged to follow them. The only thing hidden is
what they will all add up to.

Every single conversation—no matter how cordial, or casual, or brief—develops in this manner. Even in the friendliest of chats, or the smallest of small talk, one person is manipulating the other. It may not be for sinister motives, of course, and sometimes the role of manipulator will switch back and forth several times in the course of a conversation. But there is always *someone* putting in the numbered dots.

Perhaps the most striking example of this process in operation can be found in former President Richard Nixon's Watergate tapes. The transcripts of the president's conversations still make fascinating reading—not so much because of what they reveal about criminal activity being plotted in the Oval Office—but because of what they reveal about Nixon's skill, most of the time, in managing to avoid directly implicating himself in that activity. He was content to sit back and toss out the numbered dots, while his aides obligingly drew in the lines that connected them. In the end, not surprisingly, they went to jail and he didn't.

The moral: When somebody dangles a numbered dot before you in conversation, have a good look at it before you start drawing a line to it.

This principle applies even to the shortest, sharpest exchanges. A good example is the time a few years ago when British Prime Minister Harold Wilson, campaigning for re-election, was interrupted in the middle of a speech by a heckler shouting, "Rubbish!" Rather than dealing with the *implied* cry—"You're a liar!" or "You're a fool!"—Wilson deliberately directed his attention to the simple phenomenon of a man standing up in the middle of a speech and calling out the name of a certain kind of material. Smiling tolerantly, Wilson assured him: "I'll get to your special interest in a moment, sir."

Now, contrast this with the way Vice-President

Nelson Rockefeller handled an almost identical situation a couple of years later. Rockefeller, like Wilson, was making a speech when a heckler interrupted him. Unlike Wilson, however, Rockefeller ignored the heckler's explicit message—thereby forfeiting the opportunity to deal with it effectively—and instead heard the insult implicit in the message. That is to say, he saw the number beside the dot. He became so enraged at the heckler that words failed him and he let his finger do the talking. The result, of course, was exactly what the heckler wanted: Rockefeller came across as a coarse buffoon lacking in self-control.

So, once again: Always listen carefully to what is said to you. *Verbatim*. Don't let any of the words get lost in emotional translation. As you will see, they can come in very handy when it's your turn to speak.

Six Ways of Speaking Softly While Carrying A Big Stick

All right, you're in conversation and someone addresses you with the verbal equivalent of a ticking parcel. What do you do to keep it from blowing up in your face?

It depends, of course, on the precise contents of the parcel, but basically there are two alternative strategies open to you: Either (1) you contrive not to be at home when the parcel is delivered, or (2) you send it back with postage due. Put more bluntly, you can either take a soft-line or a hard-line approach. In some cases, it's better to turn away challenges gently; in other cases you may have to opt for a tougher approach. It doesn't matter which you choose as long as it works. With the hard-line approach, the object is to beat your antagonists at their own game. With the soft-line approach, you refuse to play their game at all.

To take the soft-line approach first: There are no fewer than six basic ways of going AWOL whenever you sense the possibility of a war of words. All of them have been proven to be reliable—and all of them have proven that the only thing more frustrating than a moving target is no target at all.

The first might be called the Radio Moscow technique: You jam the other fellow's transmitter with your own signals. The idea here is that you don't have to worry about answering questions or charges that never get through in the first place. A memorable instance of this kind of preemptive strike happened some years ago to a coed at Trinity College, Dublin. She was determined to interview Samuel Beckett. Beckett, as she and the world knew, was even more determined not to be interviewed. Undaunted, she went to Paris and camped out on the writer's doorstep, confident that sooner or later he would give in. Sure enough, after a couple of days Beckett relented and agreed to an interview—on the condition that it be conducted over lunch so that he could get back to work in the afternoon.

Throughout lunch at a nearby cafe Beckett peppered her with eager questions about herself, her background, her ambitions. And, eagerly, she told him everything he wanted to know. It wasn't until afterward that it dawned on her that he had given her the material for a sweet anecdote but not an interview.

Beckett understood, and skillfully exploited, the most fundamental principle of human intercourse: When it comes down to it, people are always more interested in themselves than they are in you.

The second technique is to succumb to tactical confusion. Suddenly, inexplicably, you have difficulty understanding what has been said to you. A classic example of this ploy occurred at a tender moment in the film *Annie Hall*. Woody Allen, in response to Diane Keaton's anguished late-night call, had gallantly come over and rid her apartment of "a major spider." Then, as they were cuddling in the aftermath of this trauma, she asked him, with more than passing interest, if he had had a woman in bed with him when she called. As, of course, her suspicions in the matter were extremely well-founded, Allen's face instantly froze into a mask of abject bewilderment. "What do you mean?" he asked.

What do you mean? That was possibly the funniest line in a film laced with funny lines. Not just because it was so marvelously redundant—it was impossible for him *not* to know what she meant—but because it reverberated with the echoes of a million other sticky situations. Indeed, if the chronically guilty among us were ever to form a secret society, their password would surely have to be: "Whaddayamean?"

Funnier still, the line almost always works. The other person may have spent hours laying out the numbered dots to entrap you, but the moment you insert your own dot into the picture—"What do you mean?"—suddenly it's the inquisitor who's drawing the connecting lines. Because not even the most single-minded questioner can resist the temptation to elaborate on the original question, or to justify it, or to betray the observation that prompted it.

Thus, the most loaded question can be defused and rendered harmless. "Where did you go last night?" becomes "I called at nine-thirty and there was no answer." "Are you attracted to her?" becomes "Every time I looked up you were talking to her." And so forth.

As long as you have "What do you mean?" with you, you can always trade in an awkward question for a new one, one that's easier to handle.

Another technique, similar to exhibiting confusion, is to *sow* confusion. In short, talk nonsense. People seldom linger long in the presence of looniness. For instance, to the leering predator who corners you at a party and asks what you're doing afterwards, you might say, earnestly: "Do rainy days and Sundays make you blue?" Or to the bore who is intent on prying information out of you ("Are you Jewish?" "Are you married?") you could say: "No, I'm on a Fulbright." Never underestimate the power of non sequiturs to cloud men's minds.

In dealing with more aggressive types, one of the most successful methods down through the ages has been what Jesus called turning the other cheek and what Muhammad Ali re-christened the rope-a-dope: You stand there and let your enemy flail away until he exhausts himself.

Suppose somebody comes up and accuses you of being "a scheming bastard." "I agree," you say, "but I'm curious to know which of my schemes you have in mind." Or: "You're the laziest person I know." You reply: "I'm sure that's true. When did you first begin to notice?" And once your accuser has climbed on to his own hook, you can keep him there for as long as you like. Whenever you see him beginning to wriggle off it, just encourage him to inventory your other faults. He will almost certainly be unable to decline the invitation.

This technique, it must be said, does require considerable patience. Still, that patience will be amply rewarded if you enjoy witnessing death by a thousand cuts, especially self-inflicted ones.

For those without the time or stamina for such a potentially lengthy procedure, there is a speeded-up version of this method known as one-downmanship. Instead of merely submitting cheerfully to somebody's harangue, you join in and show that nobody has more contempt for your behavior than you do. Say, for example, someone approaches you and says, "That was a filthy thing you did to X." Equally outraged, you reply, as if you were talking about somebody else, "You think *that* was bad. You should have seen what I did to Y. Terrible. What's worse, I seemed to enjoy every minute of it. It's a wonder I have any friends left. And how do I treat them when they come to me for the tiniest favor? You wouldn't *believe*. . . ."

Finally, there is the last word in soft-line deterrents: muteness. If you're not sure how to respond to a challenge, remember thát you have the option of not responding at all. No one was ever beaten in a debate that he didn't take part in. (At the same time, people *have* condemned themselves out of their own mouths when they found, to their frustration, that other lips were sealed.) So don't worry about how people will react if you are conveniently struck dumb. Even Lenin, the great epigrammatist of theoretical combat, could only recommend an appropriate course of action for those encountering mush and those encountering steel; he had no wisdom to impart to those encountering absolutely nothing.

The Harder They Fall

Then there are the hard lines: counterpunch lines for those who aren't content with merely winning a decision on points. Here is where it becomes critically important that you catch all of the words flung at you, for they will determine the precise form of your response in any given situation. The principle is the same as in judo. You let your opponent supply all the force; you just redirect it.

A remarkable display of this principle in action was provided a few years ago by the aging tennis player Bobby Riggs in his challenge match with Margaret Court. Riggs, faced with a younger and stronger opponent, wisely made no attempt to overpower Court. Rather, he met her booming volleys with an assortment of topspin lobs and junk shots until, rattled and frustrated, she began to make dreadful errors. Soon thereafter she lost control of her game entirely. It was a sad humiliation for a nice lady, but it was also a marvelous demonstration of the strategy of exploiting your opponent's strength.

You can do the very same thing—with the same results—in conversation. And, just as in tennis, you will find that it's the hard-hitting serve-and-volley types who are most vulnerable to the lobbed return.

The actual technique involved is startlingly simple. All you have to do, once the conversational ball is in your court, is to apply a certain amount of perverse literalism before returning it. Every question, every accusation, every insult is propelled by an internal logic of its own. Provided that you hear exactly what is being said to you, it's a relatively easy matter to set that logic spinning back on itself. So when the ball arrives back in your adversary's court, it not only lands in an unexpected spot but also takes a funny bounce.

The classic model for the perverse literal reply is the traditional Yiddish retort, where what has been said is twisted out of shape and returned as a question. Examples:

Close the door! It's cold outside.
If I close the door it will be warm outside?

This letter needs another stamp. It's too heavy.
If I put another stamp on it, it will get lighter?

Did you take a bath today?
Why? Is one missing?

Retorts such as these, amusing as they are, do not require great wit, or even a sense of humor. All they require is the ability to hear what people actually say, rather than what they mean to say, and the ability to take what they've said literally (if perversely).

A particularly delightful instance of perverse literalism at work is the old story of the farmer who is engaged in conversation by a passing stranger. The stranger wants to know if the farmer was born and raised in the area, so he asks: "Have you lived here all your life?" To which the old farmer replies, with splendid accuracy: "Not yet." Another often-quoted example involves the notorious bank robber, Willie Sutton. A questioner was curious to know what had made Sutton decide to become a criminal, so he enquired: "Why do you rob banks?" Sutton looked at him quizzically for a moment and then answered: "Because that's where the money is."

But the examples are endless, and in their incarnation as jokes, endlessly familiar ("Waiter, what's this fly doing in my soup?" "Looks like the breast-stroke, sir.") It's the *strategy* they exemplify that is unfamiliar. It *must* be unfamiliar, otherwise why would so many clever, witty, and amusing people often find themselves not knowing what to say to people who are anything *but* clever, or witty, or amusing? And yet the strategy for dealing with such people has been around as long as language itself. It only seems unfamiliar because at some stage in our evolution a good practice—listening to what is left unsaid—became a bad habit—*not* listening to what is *said*.

Unfortunately, however, this bad habit is seldom if ever recognized as the crippling handicap that it is. Indeed, in the interests of "honest communication," many psychologists will tell you that when you hear the lion's roar you should stick your head in the lion's mouth—on the grounds that, however painful the consequences may be for you, this will bring out into the open the nature of your relationship to the lion. Hence this bit of advice from a psychologist writing in a respected psychology journal:

When a questioner has us in his clutches, we can break the spell by paying careful attention to the speaker's tone of voice, gestures, and other hints to see what the real message is, and then respond to that deeper meaning.

It could work like this. "Where were you so late last night?" might be answered, "You seem quite worried about it," a response which opens the door for a discussion of what is really bothering the questioner.

Exactly. The only problem is that any sane person, faced with a questioner who demands to know his whereabouts at a certain time, would prefer to *shut* the door on such an interrogation. Most of us have better things to do with our time than to spend it accounting for our movements the night before. That is why it's important to understand the fundamentals of verbal self-defense. It is not so that you can devastate those who would insult or embarrass or intimidate you— although you can do that, too, if you wish—but so that you can swiftly discourage them from carrying on in a manner that wastes your time or causes you distress. Distress, even more than dishonesty, is the enemy of good conversation. And any enemy of good conversation is a wholly unnecessary evil.

As Winston Churchill once said, on being shown around a Depression-ravaged slum in the 1930s: "What a life for these poor people—never eating anything good, never making anything beautiful, never saying anything clever."

This book will not show you how to say something clever. Its sole purpose is to show you how to cut off others who are determined to say something stupid, or grumpy, or nasty. Thus, it will help you to prevent their stupidity, or grumpiness, or nastiness from dominating the conversation. An ambush is better than a shoot-out. Especially since the shoot-out would be on the other person's terms.

A Little Target Practice

How do these different strategies actually work in conversation? Well, let's consider for a moment that most intimidating of snarled questions, *"What do you think you're doing?"* It's easy to see why this is an evergreen in the repertoire of parents, teachers, cops, drill sergeants, and other authority figures. Just by turning the volume control up or down they can make the question sound like "Look at the mess you've made" or "Stop that at once" or "If you do that again you'll be punished." Consequently, you respond by excusing or justifying yourself: "I couldn't help it . . ." or "It was an accident . . ." or "I'm sorry, I didn't mean to . . ." or "I was just trying to. . . ."

Wrong, all wrong. Unless, of course, you *want* to "open the door" to someone who comes up to you and says: "What do you think you're doing?" But assuming that you don't, here are some of the various ways you have of turning aside a nasty question like that.

Among the soft-line techniques, we can disregard the first and the last. Jamming is useful only with predictable bores because it is based on the ability to anticipate what they will say. Silence speaks for itself.

That brings us, first of all, to tactical confusion as a ploy. You don't understand the question. This is most suitably rendered as: "I don't understand the question." Or you could say, very slowly, with an expression of intense bewilderment: "Pardon me?" Or you could always fall back on the classic: "What do you mean?"

The next technique is to create confusion where a moment ago there was nothing but anger or exasperation. For this, any non sequitur will do. You might say, in a hushed, conspiratorial voice: "You know, I can *prove* that Oswald had accomplices." Or you could say: "Shhh, you'll wake the baby!" (provided, of course, that there is no sleeping infant within earshot). Don't be afraid to try out your ad lib talents: Anything, as long as it's totally irrelevant, will suffice to throw your antagonist off balance.

Then there is The Other Cheek. Someone looms over you, demanding: "What do you think you're doing?" You answer, with warm sincerity, "A good question, but more importantly: What do *you* think I'm doing? . . . Oh, really? Why do you think I would want to do that? . . . In your opinion, am I the sort of person who does this often? . . . Would you say I probably derive some obscure pleasure from doing this? . . . Why is that? . . ." Et cetera, ad infinitum.

Just beyond this, there is the one-down position, the role of the enthusiastic flagellant: "What do I think I'm doing? God knows. Ever since I was lobotomized I haven't been able to do anything right. Why, just the other day. . . ." Something along those lines.

Now we come to the more subtly destructive replies—the ones that are lobbed back with reverse spin on them. They are as numerous and varied as the people and situations with which you may be confronted, and none should be thought of as The Ultimate Comeback. The ultimate comeback is, quite simply (and quite literally), the last one you have to use to rid yourself of a pest. It doesn't matter how hard or soft the line you take. All that matters is that it works.

Bearing that in mind, there are several lines that immediately suggest themselves in response to the question: "What do you think you're doing?"

Think? You expect me to THINK *about it?*

Annoying you. How's it working?

About seventy-five. Going too fast for you?

Cagney. Want to see my Edward G. Robinson?

Just fine, thanks. And you?

I give up. What?

And so on. You get the idea.

Between the Lines: Things to Remember

Now that you've got the idea, don't let go of it. For the idea is as important as the lines themselves. Admittedly, without the lines the idea wouldn't exist. However, that doesn't mean you should approach them as you would lines in a script, as something to memorize so that you can stand around waiting for your cue. You could be waiting a long time. Bullies and bores don't always follow the script. Moreover, even supposing that you had the stamina and inclination to commit to memory every single line in this book, you would sooner or later find yourself in the dreaded presence of someone who refuses to be deterred by one or two good lines. Then what? If you had been depending exclusively on those one or two lines to save you, you would probably reach for the panic button. On the other hand, as long as you have a firm grip on the strategies those lines represent, you will be able to adapt your tactics, quickly and decisively, so as to handle the most relentless of conversational bombardiers.

Nor should you go through this book expecting to find a supply of *bon mots*. In the first place, as Aldous Huxley wrote in *Point Counter Point,* "There are not enough *bon mots* in existence to provide any industrious conversationalist with a new stock for every social occasion." In the second place, the point of the exercise is not to turn you into a master of witty repartee. You need much more than an arsenal of clever ripostes—however sparkling and however well-rehearsed—to be genuinely witty in conversation. The point is to provide you with an insurance policy that will offer permanent protection against interrogation, intimidation, boredom, and other man-made disasters.

In this regard, it should be stressed again that the lines in this book—both hard and soft—are lines of *defense,* not lines of attack or even counterattack. They are strategic moves which you can use to extricate yourself, with a minimum of effort, from unpleasant situations. They are designed to help you *avoid* obnoxious, tedious people—not to make you one of them. It is up to you to decide whether a particular response is appropriate to the situation: that is, whether it is likely to achieve the desired result. Just remember that you're not shooting blanks—and it can be as risky to resort to overkill as to go around unarmed in the first place.

Given that proviso, you should not be timid about using these lines—or, better still, ones of your own devising—whenever somebody takes a verbal shot at you. The only way you will learn which lines work best for you is by trying them out. And it's the only way that others will learn what to expect if they annoy you. Besides, the cleverest line in the world isn't going to help you if you keep it to yourself.

So speak up! Any time you're tempted to let someone get away from a line that does you an injustice or injury, just keep in mind the famous—though surely apocryphal—last words of Pancho Villa, as the bullet-riddled revolutionary lay dying in the arms of a comrade.

"Don't let it end like this," he whispered. "Say I said something."

1

Accusations
and
Threats

YOU DON'T KNOW WHAT YOU'RE TALKING ABOUT

This is really one of the most unpleasant and arrogant accusations that can be leveled at you. Even if it happens to be true, there is still no justification for anyone's expressing his or her disagreement with you in such disagreeable terms. However misinformed you may be—and that has not yet been proven—or however misdirected your arguments, it is most unlikely that you are guilty as charged. Consider: If you were as comprehensively ignorant as your accuser suggests, you would hardly have been in a position to say something so splendidly provocative as to call forth this aggressive reaction.

Be that as it may, it would be a serious mistake, as always, to focus on the legitimacy of the accusation. That in itself lends it a certain modicum of legitimacy. Worse, it tugs the conversation toward a discussion of what you know and don't know: That way disaster lies unless you know a lot more than you're letting on. Rather, you should concentrate on the statement itself, and then adjust your response according to the sort of effect you want to achieve.

For example, if the remark was made without
particular malice, you might shrug it off playfully:

> *I was hoping you wouldn't notice.*

> *Would it make any difference if I did?*

If it was made more in sorrowful confusion
than in anger you could add a confusing twist
of your own:

> *Do* YOU?

If, however, you detect an undertow of scorn
(and you probably will), you can put a little
sting in the tail of your reply:

> *You're right. I guess I thought with you it
> wouldn't matter.*

> *True, we do have that in common.*

But perhaps the remark was as much designed
to humiliate you in front of others as it was to
draw attention to your supposed inadequacy.
In which case you should reply, softly, smil-
ingly:

> *If you prefer, I could talk about something
> I DO know about. Your manners, for ex-
> ample.*

I WOULDN'T DO THAT IF I WERE YOU

Here is a threat positively oozing menace, one that implies the direst of consequences if you proceed with whatever it is that you are doing. But look again, closely. If the consequences will be so dire, why aren't they spelled out—or even hinted at? More tellingly, why does the threatener refer to himself twice as often as he refers to you—and in a hypothetical situation, at that?

There are two possible reasons. On the one hand, he may not have made up his mind what the consequences will be, and he is waiting for you to make it up for him. On the other hand, it may be that his vocabulary is too small to carry the full weight of the anger, frustration, rage, or whatever else prompted the threat.

Either way, he wants to buy time to fit his words to his feelings. Sell it to him:

> *Why not?*

> *What* WOULD *you do if you were me?*

Whatever his answer, you are now in the driver's seat. Even if he simply repeats or rephrases the threat, and even if you decide to heed its warning, you are still in the triumphant position of being able to point out that you are only doing what *he* would do.

Another approach you can take, if you think the threat might best be doused by splashing silliness over it, is to treat it as a confession calling for sympathy and encouragement:

> *But think of the excitement you would miss.*

> *It would be difficult at first, but you'd*
> *eventually get the hang of it.*

Or you can be silly and discouraging:

> *I certainly hope not.*

Or silly and superior:

> *It's all right—I know how.*

Finally, if you think it's wise in the circumstances, you can simply and bluntly meet the threat head-on:

> *I don't blame you.*

> *If I were you, I wouldn't either.*

YOU'RE NOT GOING TO GET AWAY WITH THAT!

Now we go from Subjunctive Threat to Future Threat, trading in hypothesis for prediction. The new form, however, serves exactly the same purpose as the old: It acts as a temporary release for the threatener's anger while he tries to decide what he's going to do about it. After all, if he really thought that you weren't going to "get away with" something or other, why would he take the trouble to notify you in advance? Again, he needs time to think—and he needs you to say something that will clarify and, he hopes, justify his anger.

Don't. Stay with the cards that have already been dealt.

If you feel that prudence calls for you to fold your hand, you can do it with satirical grace:

> *You know, you may be on to something there.*

> *Just my luck.*

In most instances, though, you will find it more rewarding to play the trumps you hold as a result of the threat's promissory aspect:

> How do you know? Have you already tried?

> Who is, then?

More succinctly, maddeningly:

> *When?*

I DON'T SEE WHAT DIFFERENCE IT MAKES TO YOU

Whenever you hear an accusation masquerading as an admission, as in this case, you have your accuser exactly where you want him, so long as you join in the masque.

At the most basic level, there is the deadpan acknowledgment:

> *I know you don't.*

> *Obviously.*

Turning up the heat a little, you can make the acknowledgment more explicit by tacking on an admission of your own:

> It DOESN'T *make any difference to me.*
> *But it's not me I'm worried about.*

There's also the sort of "clarification" designed to sow confusion:

> *If I thought you did, I wouldn't have said anything.*

Confusing, too, is an expression of innocent curiosity:

> *What* DO *you see?*

For sheer impact, though, it's hard to beat this simple directive, followed by a slowly forming, thoroughly malevolent grin:

> *Look again.*

YOU THINK YOU'RE SO CLEVER

One of the things about accusations that people find most troubling is that they follow no set pattern. They come in all shapes and sizes—depending on the emotional shape of the accuser and the size of his vocabulary. This, however, can work to your advantage, because it means that you can usually impose your own shape on the accusation.

With this one, for example, you may wish to treat it as an order:

> *Okay. Tell me when to start.*

Or as a suggestion:

> *That's a splendid idea. But what will* YOU *think about?*

Or as a question:

> *No, but keep talking. You may yet convince me.*

Or as a simple observation, with which you may be moved to agree:

> *You do have that effect on me.*

You may even care to explain how you arrived at the thought:

> *But only by process of elimination. I tried thinking* YOU *were clever and it just didn't work.*

GET OUT OF MY WAY!

Threats, like accusations, take many different forms. Therefore, like accusations, they can generally be forced into whatever form you find easiest to deal with. Consider the above threat: It is not really a threat at all unless you assume an elipsis is trailing in its wake

(". . . or I'll knock your block off"). It could just as well be advice about some entertainment treat you may have missed.

In which case you respond accordingly:

> *"Out of My Way"? I haven't heard of it, but if you say it's good. . . .*

Or it could be the first in a series of urgent requests:

> *Right. Then what?*

If, on the other hand, it appears that you are being given notice to evacuate a particular area, it would certainly be proper for you to try to ascertain the precise boundaries of the area in question:

> *Which way is yours?*

Or you can go straight to the first problem raised by the act of getting out of his way:

> *Whose way should I get in?*

HOW COULD YOU DO SUCH A THING?

The *intended* accusation, of course, is: "You must have no sense of decency (or tact, or morality, or whatever) to be able to do such a thing." But bad intentions, like good ones, have a way of getting lost before they reach the real world. The intention to accuse here is a case in point. Somewhere down the line it picked up a question mark, so that when it arrives in the conversation it sounds exactly like a request for information.

You should honor that request. Perhaps by divulging the secret of your success:

> *A lot of practice.*

> *I try harder.*

Perhaps by indicating the range of your competence:

> *Oh, lots of different ways. I just happen to like this one.*

Perhaps by indicating the range of your stamina:

> *Repeatedly, if need be.*

Perhaps by assessing your relative ability:

> *Better than most people.*

Perhaps by simply showing your willingness to please:

> *Any way you like. What's your favorite?*

YOU CAN'T REALLY MEAN THAT

Of course you can mean it. There's even a good chance that you *do* mean it. But the important thing is that your accuser knows this already. The reason he gives you a chance to reconsider is to give *himself* a chance to come up with an appropriate response. But you don't reconsider what you said. You reconsider what *he* said.

This might leave you in a state of tactical bewilderment:

> *That's funny. I could have sworn I meant it.*

Or tactical insecurity:

> *I must be slipping. I always used to mean it.*

Perhaps you would feel better confessing, to get it over with:

> *You're right. I just made it up.*

Or you may not be able to restrain your curiosity as to the origins of his insight:

> *What tipped you off?*

In any event, it's a rare opportunity to point out one of the more rewarding aspects of being around people in the accusing business:

> *I don't have to mean it. I can get the same reaction just by saying it.*

YOU'RE A LIAR!

This is one of those rare accusations that come right at you, without any semantic camouflage and often without any warning. What to do? Plead guilty. Immediately. Once you've done that, you have taken the initiative away from your accuser and put him on the defensive. All that remains to be done is to choose what sort of twist to give your confession.

An especially satisfying twist, having testified against yourself, is to cast doubt on the reliability of your testimony:

> *I admit it. But then, of course, I could be lying.*

A variation:

> *True. Or false. Who knows with me?*

Another effective ploy is to raise the specter of unequal justice:

> *So was Nixon, and you voted for* HIM.

This is not to say that you have to apologize for being a liar. Lying is, after all, our one truly creative pastime. So don't hesitate to show pride in your talent, at the same time offering encouragement to someone manifestly less talented:

> *With a little imagination, you could be, too.*

TAKE THAT BACK!

The idea, presumably, is that you should deny having meant to say what you just said. And like most silly ideas, it has found a form to match. In this instance it is a request for you to accept the return of something already delivered.

You may wish to express your reluctance:

> *No, please, it's on me.*

Or your disappointment:

> *Pity. It was such a perfect fit.*

Or your puzzlement:

> *So soon? You haven't even had time to enjoy it.*

> *But then what would I do with it?*

Or, finally, your acquiescence:

> *Okay, but any time you need it just let me know.*

IF YOU KNOW WHAT'S GOOD FOR YOU . . .

Your response to this threat will be determined largely by your timing. If you can get a word in before the threat goes any further, you ought to be able to cut it off at the pass. The word, of course, should name something good for you:

> *Vitamins.*

> *Vegetables.*

In all likelihood, however, you will have the full threat to deal with. In which case you should be candid:

> *If I knew what was good for me, I wouldn't be here.*

Or fatalistic:

> *True, but I'm self-destructive.*

Alternatively, you might find it worthwhile to indulge in quiet speculation as to the source of this unsolicited advice:

> *You haven't by any chance been talking to my mother, have you?*

I DIDN'T APPRECIATE THAT!

Looming in the shadowy distance behind this threat, out of earshot, is something along the lines of: "I'm angry with you for saying (or doing) what you did, and I'm warning you not to do it again." Still, what you hear is what you get. What you have here is a frank admission of inadequacy or of a failure to appreciate something.

You can call attention to this failure by attempting to gauge its extent:

> *Not even a little bit?*

Or you can hint that it may be symptomatic of a more comprehensive failure:

> *What sort of things* DO *you appreciate?*

Perhaps the failure is simply one of effort:

> *You didn't even try.*

Or perhaps it is due to the novelty of the experience:

> *It's an acquired taste.*

> *You'll grow into it.*

Anway, be cheering and charitable:

> *It's always hard the first time.*

YOU ACTUALLY ENJOY DOING THAT, DON'T YOU?

Of all the sins that one might commit, by far the worst—in the eye of the accuser—is to be conspicuously lacking in remorse for one's sinfulness. Amateur prosecutors can put up with almost anything but a refusal to feel guilty. Thus, as here, they are often driven to attack your behavior in terms of your motives. This is an open invitation for you to expand on the wicked pleasure you seem to be getting.

You may choose to deny that pleasure is in any way involved:

> *No, I lost an election bet.*

Or you may experience the first dawning of pleasure:

> *I'm beginning to.*

> *Now that you mention it, I do get kind of a thrill out of it.*

Or you may wish to place it in your scale of pleasurable activities:

> *Not as much as setting fire to cats, but it'll do.*

And you can always qualify it:

> *Only when people notice.*

STEP OUTSIDE AND REPEAT THAT!

Considering that this threat implies physical violence, you would do well to remember that however brilliant your retort, should it lead to a broken nose it cannot be deemed altogether successful. On the other hand, if your adversary really wanted an immediate, face-to-face showdown, why would he feel compelled to request a change of venue?

These considerations aside, the literal request is for you to say again something you've already said, but at another location. This could be due to the other person's inability to hear you:

> *It is noisy in here, isn't it? What I said was. . . .*

Or to the person's eagerness to remember your words accurately:

> *Like it, huh?*

> *I'm frightened of the dark. Would it be all right if I just wrote it down for you?*

You could decline graciously:

> *I couldn't possibly. I was taught that it's bad manners to repeat myself.*

Or somewhat less graciously:

> *I'm busy right now. Why don't YOU step outside and repeat that?*

In any case, no mention has been made of anyone accompanying you outside:

> *What? And miss all the fun of being inside talking to you?*

I'M SICK AND TIRED OF YOUR . . .

This is a sick and tired way of saying: "Stop it!" However, it comes out as a vague medical bulletin, and so should be treated as such. You might respond with an expression of diagnostic concern:

> *Which came first, the sickness or the tiredness?*

> *Both sick* AND *tired? You ought to see a specialist about that.*

Or with a sudden recognition of the symptoms:

> *You know, I* THOUGHT *you were looking a bit older.*

Or with an uplifting reminder that things could be worse:

> *Just think how bad you'd feel if I had been taking you seriously.*

Or with a consoling thought:

> *You're probably only sick because you're tired.*

Or with merciful concurrence:

> *Me too. Let's talk about* YOUR. . . .

ARE YOU GOING TO ANSWER MY QUESTION?

Congratulations. Since this growled enquiry always rides on the coattails of some kind of inquisitorial demand, you have already scored a major triumph by getting your inquisitor to shift his focus to the inquisition itself. Now all you have to do in order to consolidate your superior position is to keep the focus locked on the follow-up question.

You can do it teasingly:

> *I doubt it. But it's too early to say for sure.*

Or testingly, by means of a hopeful scenario:

> *Will you get mad and leave if I say no?*

On the other hand, you might want to meet the implied threat with an implied threat of your own:

> *If you're lucky, no.*

Or you can turn it inside out, imposing a condition along the way:

> *If you promise not to question my answer.*

Or you can deliver the sought-after
confirmation in such a way as to satisfy the
question without satisfying the questioner:

> *Most definitely. I'll get a letter off to you
> in the morning.*

I HEARD THAT!

Whatever it was that they heard—a *sotto voce* retort, a
mumbled invocation, a grumbled aside—you mustn't
appear in any way alarmed. The best way not to appear alarmed is to appear pleased:

> *You were meant to.*

Or at least chronically unfazed:

> *It doesn't surprise me. You're always
> hearing things.*

And there is always casual curiosity:

> *Really? What did it sound like?*

Well, almost certainly it sounded like an insult—you knew this already—so you might
care to validate the perception, adding visuals
to the audial impression:

> *Very good. Now let's see how you do on
> this one. . . .*

Then you put your thumbs in your ears, wig-
gle your fingers, grin broadly, and stick out
your tongue.

Finally, considering the possibility—indeed
the likelihood—that the overheard remark
was directed at a third party, you might wish
to bounce your response off that third party,
in a designed-to-be-overheard stage whisper:

> *Ever since he started cleaning his ears I
> haven't had a moment's peace.*

YOU'RE HIDING SOMETHING FROM ME

Anyone who levels an accusation like this is on a
fishing expedition. True, he has spotted a ripple on the
surface of your conversation, but he doesn't really
know what caused it. Therefore, he had to bait his
hook with this all-purpose worm.

Don't bite. Nibble:

> *Depends on what you mean by "some-
> thing."*

Or tantalize him with a quick splash:

> *I have no choice. I can't very well hide it
> from myself.*

Or give him warning that you are about to become The One That Got Away:

> *I know, but I'm not finished yet. Close
> your eyes and count to a hundred.*

Then again, you may want to show your contempt for such crude bait:

> *Only my boredom.*

But perhaps you're willing to play the game:

> *Right. Bet you can't guess which hand it's in.*

Still, even in a game, there are rules to be observed:

> *You weren't supposed to peek.*

I KNOW YOUR TYPE

Unless you've been keeping a profile so low that you must have been ducking, there are a lot of people out there who think they know your type. And they've been waiting a long time for the chance to ambush you. Thus, again, the key element in your reaction is a conspicuous lack of surprise.

This can take the form of a simple query:

> *Often?*

Or a simple acknowledgment of the importance of your type:

> *Some people have all the luck.*

But if you want to get clinical about it:

> *AB negative. How'd you know?*

Or boastful:

> *You must be from a good family.*

Or just relieved:

> *Thank heavens. You'd be surprised how many people I have to explain it to.*

DON'T GET SMART WITH ME!

Strangely, but conveniently, almost every intentionally nasty adjective employed by threateners and accusers is either unintentionally complimentary or loaded with ambiguity on its flip side. What, for example, is the opposite of smartness in the vernacular? You've got it:

> *Okay, I'll be dumb.*

And when you follow that line with total silence—dumbness—you've pulled off the double: a spoken put-down trailed by a silent pun.

But let's get back to the smartness—and the "witness"—that occasioned the threat:

> *I didn't think it was possible to get smart with you.*

And although it may *not* be possible, it's still worth trying:

> *But it's so boring when we're both on the same level.*

Yet it's a level that has its own compensations:

> *Even if I do, you'll never know.*

Though perhaps it's best to make your exit from the conversation—at this level—by permission:

> *Mind if I get smart on my own?*

2
Insults

YOU SHOULD THINK BEFORE YOU SPEAK

There's one thing that has to be said for insults: However nasty, mean, vindictive, personal, cruel, surprising, or shocking they may be, they are *always* pathetic. There are no exceptions. An insult is the retarded offspring of a brief and torrid romance between a simple mind and a lazy tongue (or a lazy mind and a simple tongue, as the case may be). Consequently, and gratifyingly, these miserable creatures do not live very long if they are dipped into the icy waters of logic and literalism.

Consider the above example. Since it is quite impossible *not* to think before you speak, you must assume that the real burden of the message is buried in one of its parts.

Perhaps it's a question of timing, with the emphasis on "before":

But then what would I do afterwards?

59

Perhaps as a listener your tendency to meditate is unsettling:

> *I'll try. It's just that I'm so used to thinking before* YOU *speak.*

Or perhaps it's your habit of thinking at unscheduled, unproductive times:

> *I agree. It does make more sense than thinking before I go to the bathroom.*

But at some stage you will have to confront the tiresome possibility that your insulting companion is actually proposing that you should think before you speak. Take him up on his proposal by all means, but first you ought to test his sincerity:

> *Why should I have an unfair advantage?*
>
> *You sure you wouldn't feel left out?*

Finally, though, the most economical way of dealing with this insult is with an inscrutable smile—and sepulchral silence. Later, usually not more than a couple of seconds later, when your nonplussed adversary is compelled to break the silence, you quickly cut him off:

> *Sshhh. I'm thinking.*

DIDN'T YOUR MOTHER EVER TEACH YOU ANY MANNERS?

Whatever you've done to attract this particular insult, you may well be wondering what your mother did to earn a part in it. Nothing. She was imported under the conversational law that permits relatives and ancestors to be brought into a discussion for the purpose of converting an accusation into an insult. Such rhetorical devices are meant to fluster you, to provoke you into the sort of outburst that will lend *ex post facto* credibility to the insult.

Don't take the bait. Instead, play with it:

I'm an orphan.

Or consider it pityingly for a moment, and then walk away from it:

I really don't remember. I'm afraid you'll have to ask HER.

Alternatively, you can tie a knot in it and hand it back:

Some. She taught me it was rude to ask questions like that.

Yes. All bad, unfortunately.

Maybe even a couple of knots:

No, she was like yours in that respect.

WHY DON'T YOU GROW UP?

One of the hallmarks of the insult is the use of the inter-
rogative form which turns an unwelcome observation
into an unanswerable question. It is also one of the
things that certify the inherent ludicrousness of an insult.
Just as a clock doesn't need a cuckoo in order to give
you the time, a person doesn't need to resort to a ridiculous question in order to give you an opinion. But the
cuckoo is on your side. You see, it's really a homing
pigeon in disguise. All you have to do is wrap a message
around its spindly legs and let it find its way home.

You might, for instance, send it back with a
request for clarification:

> *As opposed to growing* DOWN?

> *You mean rather than growing radishes?*

Or with earnest speculation:

> *Could be my diet: I eat a lot of junk foods.*

> *I started smoking when I was six.*

But probably the most satisfying way is to send
it back by way of California:

> *I just love people who are into growth.*

I HOPE YOU WON'T TAKE THIS PERSONALLY, BUT . . .

This is not an insult in itself, but it is very often the preamble to one, usually one of a highly personal nature. So you should be prepared—whenever you hear these warning sounds—to launch a preemptive strike.

For example, you might reasonably break into the sentence to enquire:

> *Are we talking about the human condition in general, then?*

Or to clear up a basic point:

> *If I'm not supposed to take it personally, who is?*

Or to be reassuring:

> *I never take things personally. That's what I have a business manager for.*

Or to make alternative arrangements:

> *All right, I won't. I'll send somebody around to get it.*

> *Okay, let me give you my agent's phone number.* HE *can take it personally.*

I DON'T TALK TO PEOPLE LIKE YOU

If there is such a thing as an insult to be grateful for, this is it. So don't hesitate to express your gratitude:

> *Ah, my lucky day.*
>
> *Thank heaven for small mercies.*

Or at least your awareness:

> *It shows.*

Although, given the wording of the message, there may be some legitimate doubt as to whether it was addressed to you:

> *Oh, excuse me, I thought you were talking to me.*

Assuming that it *was* addressed to you, you may be excused for wondering:

> *Who keeps you company while you're shaving?*

But for lovers of symmetry, the only way to deal with an insult like this is with a timely attack of deafness:

> *What did you say? . . .*
>
> *I beg your pardon? . . .*
>
> *How's that again?*

After two or three of these, when the person who doesn't talk to people like you begins to feel the clammy grip of the irony he's talked himself into, your exit line will be there waiting:

> *Sorry, I don't seem to hear people like you.*

WHO DO YOU THINK YOU ARE?

I know: You've gone through life convinced that, if you knew nothing else, at least you knew who you were. In fact, you were more or less sure that other people knew who you were, too. And now this. Well, cheer up. By the time you've given your answer to this line both friends and foes alike will have a much better idea of who you are.

One way to handle the question is to clarify its implications:

> *You mean I have to BE someone to talk to you?*

Another is to *toy* with its implications:
I really haven't given it much thought. Do you think a lot about who YOU are?

But don't forget that there is still a whole catalog of self-images to choose from in framing your reply.

You could take the blurry one:

> *I don't know for sure. I must be somebody, though. I get a lot of mail.*

The schizophrenic one:

> *On bad days, Napoleon.*

The up-to-the-minute one:

> *Right now? A victim.*

The humble one:

> *Nobody you've heard of.*

The deliciously deluded one:

> *Him. Now ask him who he thinks* HE *is.*

THAT'S A SIX, MISS

This may not be a *prima facie* insult, but when spoken by a smirking saleslady who wants to let you know that you would be wasting your time trying to squeeze into a particular dress, it's worse than an insult. It's a vicious slur on everything you have dieted for.

Show no mercy:

> *I know, but it's so ugly I can't resist it.*

Or show that you can read:

> *So* THAT'S *what that little number on the label is there for.*

Or show that the insult was wasted on the wrong party:

> *My dog won't mind. He'll sleep on anything that's soft.*

Or show that the insult was wasted, period:

> *That's all? Maybe I should get two of them.*

Yet you can still agree with half of the saleslady's remark:

> *It may be a six. It's* DEFINITELY *a miss.*

Although it will probably be more fun to disagree with the other half:

> *Out of ten? I would have given it a three.*

WELL, EVERYONE ELSE LIKES IT

". . . and therefore there's something wrong with you for *not* liking it." That part of the insult is left blank, for you to fill in yourself. Ignore it. Instead, concentrate on the rather startling fact that the information you have been given, if true, could only have been gathered as a result of awesomely comprehensive poll-taking. How else would your insulter know the opinion of everyone else? Think about it.

Talk about it:

> *You must be exhausted after asking them all.*

Check on the gullibility factor:

> *Really? They weren't just pretending?*

Show that the information hardly comes as news:

> *I'm not surprised.*

> OF COURSE *they do! That was the idea.*

Or hint darkly at some hidden truth:

> *Yes, but did they tell you* WHY?

IS THAT THE BEST YOU CAN DO?

Nasty, nasty. Tricky, too, because if you reply in the affirmative, you are certifying your own incompetence. If you answer in the negative, you are admitting that you really *aren't* doing very well. Nevertheless, along the Yes/No continuum there are a number of stops you can make to off-load the burden of this insult.

At the affirmative end of the line:

> *Yes, I'm on piecework.*

Moving on to the conditional:

> *That remains to be seen.*

> *Stick around and you'll find out.*

Pausing at the apologetic:

> *I'm sorry. You didn't tell me you wanted the best.*

Ending up with the negative:

> *No, it's the best I NEED to do.*

Perhaps with an explanation:

> *I'm saving myself for marriage.*

GO TO HELL!

This is a fairly uncomplicated suggestion, so it's up to you to complicate it:

> *You mean this isn't it?*

You might need directions:

> *Okay, what's your address again?*

Or perhaps an added incentive:

> *What's it like there this time of year?*

Or perhaps added cash:

> *I can't afford to. Any other places you've been that you can recommend?*

Then again, it *is* an opportunity to get away from it all. Be grateful:

> *Sounds enticing. Can I give you a lift?*
>
> *Anyone I should look up for you?*

YOU MUST BE JOKING!

This line is innocent enough when used to convey incredulity or amazement. It only becomes insulting when it is converted—with the help of a scornful expression and a deliberately weary cadence—into a vehicle for ridicule or contempt. But you can do some converting of your own. Take it not as an insult but as a command, or a guess, or a speculative identification, or a cheery greeting.

If you choose to hear it as a command:

> *All right, if you say so. Did you hear the one about . . . ?*

If it's a guess, you can confirm its accuracy:

> *Of course I am.*

At the same time noting the strange solemnity that accompanied the guess:

> *True. But you still forgot to laugh.*

Or perhaps it was totally inaccurate to begin with:

> *Guess again.*

If it's a speculative identification, you may be curious to find out:

> *How can you tell?*

And if it's a cheery greeting, you should reply in kind:

> *Right! And you must be the straight man!*

DIDN'T ANYBODY EVER TELL YOU THAT . . .

Ironically, but predictably, this ill-mannered construction is almost always employed to call attention to some alleged failure of manners on *your* part. No matter. Whatever shape the complete insult takes, you already have more than enough to work with as it stands.

You can, for instance, take it as meaning that the other person has had an experience that he wants to tell you about:

> *No, what's it like to have somebody tell you that?*
>
> *I don't believe so. I suppose* YOU *must hear that a lot, though.*

Or you can explain *why* nobody has ever told you that:

> *I don't know anybody quite that rude. Do you?*

Or you may concede that someone *might* have told you:

> *Possibly, but I never listen to people who say things like that.*

Or you may recall that indeed there *was* an occasion:

> *Once, a pederast.*

HOW MUCH DO YOU CHARGE TO HAUNT A HOUSE?

Cute. Really cute. But, as ever, you should give due weight to the seriousness of the enquiry:

How many rooms?

Because the need may be more urgent than you had realized:

Oh, your mother finally moved out?

Or your friend may be trying to make a career choice:

Why? Are you out of work again?

Or, having made the choice, he wants to assess his chances of success:

Trying to find out if your rates are competitive?

Chances are, though, his rates are more than competitive:

Same as you. But I only work ONE *day a week.*

THANKS FOR NOTHING!

Not a great deal of ingenuity is required to devise suitable responses to this line:

> *Any time.*

> *Don't mention it.*

If you want to add a little decoration:

> *My pleasure, believe me.*

> *Think nothing of it.*

More elaborate still:

> *It's yours to enjoy.*

> *You don't have to thank me. You deserve it.*

Or you can give your blessing to the person who has nothing:

> *Gesundheit!*

CAN'T YOU DO ANYTHING RIGHT?

This line admirably illustrates Carroll's First Law of Insults: The more unpleasant they are, the easier they are to deal with. It must have something to do with nature's system of handicapping, whereby every predator is given a disadvantage to overcome in its search for prey. In the case of insulters, the more obnoxious ones almost always have to carry around an answer so bulky that it invariably gets in the way of their words. This leads to ridiculous lines like the one above.

You might reply by combining destiny and logic:

> *Would I be here with you if I could do anything right?*

Or by requesting further information:

> *I'm not sure. What's the first step?*

Or by providing a glimpse of your privileged situation:

> *I don't know. I've never had to.*

Or, finally, by citing some of those things you know you can do right:

> *I can get you angry whenever I want to.*

> *Yes, I'm good at avoiding bores. Excuse me for a moment.*

YOU SHOULD USE SOME COMMON SENSE

What, in effect, you are being told is that you belong in either an ivory tower or a padded cell. But let that pass. What's relevant is not the burden of the speech but the *parts* of speech. Start with the adjective:

> *I don't use* ANYTHING *that's common.*

Or, from the other direction:

>   *As opposed to* UN*common sense?*

And don't forget the noun:

>   *You mean instead of using common*
>   *drugs?*

Perhaps you would like to concentrate on the consequences of using common sense:

>   *If I did, you'd have to find someone else*
>   *to talk to.*

And, in the present company:

>   *It would make me too conspicuous.*

STILL LOOKING FOR A JOB?

This is really hitting below the belt. So don't hesitate to hit back in the same general area:

>   *Still looking for something to talk about?*

If that was your smash, here's your lob:

>   *Still looking in windows at night?*

But perhaps the line was intended as a back-handed compliment to your choice of clothes. One backhand deserves another:

>   *No, I dress like this when I'm slumming,*
>   *too.*

More stingingly:

> *Why? Is yours still available?*

Or sweetly, as you fade away:

> *Actually, I was looking for the bath-
> room.*

SURELY, EVEN YOU . . .

This is a snide cousin of "Can't you do anything right?" You might choose to meet it head-on:

Surely, even YOU *know better than to say
something like that.*

Or you can sidestep it:

> *I'm not even, I'm odd.*

Or you can ask for identification:

> *What's this? An unsolicited testimonial?*

But given the anguished tone of the insult, it might be interesting to ascertain whether your insulter's economic well-being is in some way bound up with your—even *your* —ability to perform:

> *Did you put any money on it?*

Finally, a little misunderstanding can go a long way when someone is already seething with exasperation:

My name's not Shirley.

DON'T YOU THINK YOU SHOULD BE GETTING PROFESSIONAL HELP?

Rarely do people have the courage, or the nerve, to come right out and tell you that you're crazy as a loon and somebody ought to throw a net over you. Rather, they remark on the possible desirability of your seeking "professional help."

The best way to deal with this or any other slur on your sanity is to call attention to its source:

Why? Are you going on vacation?

You could even express a modicum of bogus concern:

Wouldn't that put you out of work?

Maybe your adviser is trying to tell you something about his credentials:

You mean you're not actually licensed?

Or his feelings of remorse about the sort of
advice he's been giving:

> *Perhaps I should, if only to offset the
> professional discouragement I'm getting
> now.*

So put his small mind at rest:

> *No need to. Not with so many helpful
> amateurs around.*

WHAT'S THE MATTER WITH YOU?

Let's take the two extremes first: You can either deliver the complete and unabridged version of everything that is, or might be, or ever has been, the matter
with you—or you can shoot back with one swift sylla-
ble:

> *You.*

Moving on from cause to effect:

> *Indigestion.*

More colorfully, painfully:

> *Hemorrhoids.*

Ominously:

> *Guilt. I feel bad about killing the last
> person who asked me that.*

Fearfully:

The Ayatollah knows my address.

Still, when you have an insulter barking at
your heels, probably the simplest course is to
show him your heels:

Nothing that can't be cured by leaving.

Then leave.

3
Stupid
Questions

HOW CAN YOU STAND TO EAT THAT STUFF?

If you're lucky, you will be asked this question when your mouth is full. In which case all you need to do is utter a preliminary gurgle, then point apologetically to your bulging cheeks. And then continue to refill your mouth the moment there is a vacancy. And keep gurgling, pointing, smiling at intervals until your questioner's attention span expires.

But if you're not lucky enough to qualify for the "mouth-full" exemption, you still have three excellent ways of fielding this question. One is by accepting it on its own terms:

I can't. That's why I'm sitting down.

Easy. Have you ever tried SMOKING *it?*

Another is by taking it on *your* terms (the more disgusting the better):

I think of all the starving people in India. It gives me a big appetite.

We ran out of dog. Dumb beasts finally learned about crossing the road here.

Then again, maybe a kind of honesty is the best policy:

> *It helps if you have a bad cold.*

AM I INTERRUPTING SOMETHING?

To begin with, you can dismiss any idea of trying the obvious answer—*Yes*—because it will never deter someone who has already demonstrated an inability to pay attention to the obvious. For no one ever asks this question *unless* he is interrupting something. That's what makes it stupid.

Probably the best way to draw attention to this fact is to exploit the ambiguity in the question. You can assume that it springs from rampant narcissism:

> *I don't know. What were you doing?*

> *Sorry, I wasn't watching. Do it again and I'll try to guess.*

If, however, you are dealing with a recidivist who has proven himself to be unsusceptible to such stratagems, you can always enquire, with a weary sigh:

> *Why should today be different from any other day?*

Finally, you can employ the dirtiest of dirty
tricks by forcing him to answer his own question. You simply say:

> *Not yet.*

Then you go back to whatever you were doing.
Whether he retreats or advances, victory is
yours.

HOW DID YOU MAKE OUT LAST NIGHT?

If you haven't discovered this already, you will sooner
or later be forced to face the dispiriting fact that, as far as
most of your acquaintances are concerned, the most interesting thing about you is your sex life. This is not, sad
to say, because of your magical allure. Nor is it because
there are shimmering hints of amazing sexual prowess
woven into the fabric of your personality. It is simply,
annoyingly, because when it comes to our most intimate
behavior, people need the experience of others to fill the
gaps—real or imagined—in their own experience.

This is especially true if you are single or not otherwise paired off. It is assumed that your every waking
moment is consecrated to the pursuit of erotic happiness. Now, it may be that your every waking moment
is so consecrated; nonetheless, it is most unwise to issue
bulletins on your progress. Depending on the degree of
success you have enjoyed, you will succeed only in giving people reason to hate you or pity you.

By and large, the most effective way to deal
with an inquisitor who wants to know how you
"made out" last night is with pointed humor.
You can begin by pointing it at the inquisitorial
aspect of the question:

> *Fine, Kojak.*

> *You're not from Vice, are you?*

Or you can disqualify yourself as a witness and
shift the burden of evidence on to someone
else:

> *If he (she) is to be believed: sensationally.*

> *You know, I was having so much fun I for-
> got to ask.*

Or you can interpret the question as a blunt
inquiry into your technique. Be equally blunt:

> *Normally. None of that kinky stuff for me.*

But with the repeat offender, the one who continually requires updates on your private life,
you may need to put a slightly sharper point to
your reply. You can do this by treating the
question as if it were a pitifully straightforward
request for basic information:

> *It's much too complicated to explain in
> words. Why don't you get a book on the
> subject, one with lots of pictures?*

BY YOURSELF TONIGHT, DEAR?

This line, beloved of waiters who want to disguise (but only thinly) their disgust at the likelihood of a small tip, is guaranteed—and perhaps even intended—to spoil the appetite of any woman dining alone in a restaurant.

To help improve your appetite, you can send the question back to cook a little longer:

> *Unless you've just spotted somebody I hadn't noticed.*

Or you can send the waiter back, to ponder the wisdom of asking such a question:

> *No. Now stop being so nosy and bring Harvey some carrots.*

If the waiter has been a long time in coming, you can always consider the question as evidence of his concern about having neglected you:

> *So far—but then I KNEW the service was slow here.*

Or you could comment on the difficulty of being by yourself with a waiter present:

> *I'm trying to be. So maybe you could take my order quickly.*

Finally, there is the possibility that the waiter is asking about your hopes and plans for the immediate future:

> *If all goes well.*

ARE YOU STILL MARRIED?

People who need constant news updates on your private life usually have a singularly charming way of requesting them. Are you *still* married? Wonderful. But, like all stupid questions, it is wonderfully vulnerable to all kinds of literal misinterpretations:

> *No, I'm only still when I'm alone.*

> *Yes, we* BOTH *are as a matter of fact.*

Should you want to show your respect for the importance of precision:

> *What time is it?*

Or your lack of respect for the importance of the topic:

> *You'll have to ask my lawyer. He keeps track of such things.*

Maybe there *is* no clear-cut answer:

> *Most of the time.*

Or maybe your questioner has in mind the alternatives:

> *Yes. We thought about getting widowed but decided against it.*

WHY ISN'T YOUR HUSBAND HERE WITH YOU?

At best, this question is merely dull-witted. There are, after all, more stimulating topics of conversation than why a person is not present. At worst, when it is wrapped around an innuendo, it is insulting. Only you can decide how loaded the question is.

If you decide that it is dull but harmless, you can profess ignorance:

> *He didn't tell me.*

Or you can be kooky:

> *Someone had to stay at home with the goldfish.*

> *The full moon. He gets self-conscious.*

But if you feel that the question has snide overtones, you may want to put a small charge into your reply:

> *Because* HE *had a choice.*

> *He thought he could get bored just as easily watching TV.*

YOU SEEM SO MISERABLE. IS SOMETHING WRONG?

If you are forced to spend time with someone who asks questions like this, you have every right to be miserable. I know that's only marginally consoling, but at least such a question affords you a splendid, if brief, opportunity to cheer yourself up. One of the more amusing ways is to recite a long litany of crushing personal tragedies which are, preferably, macabre and disgustingly detailed.

Or you can pick at random from the history of disasters:

> *Didn't you hear? Archduke Ferdinand was assassinated!*

On the other hand, it may be more fun to affect bewilderment:

> *Oh, I thought I was being the life of the party.*

Even pathological bewilderment:

> *Wrong with what?*

Or to divulge a little secret:

> *It's only an act. I may* SEEM *miserable to you, but deep down I'm feeling gay and frolicky.*

Not forgetting that there are times when honesty is the best policy:

> *Now there is.*

HAVE YOU CONSIDERED THE CONSEQUENCES?

One of the least agreeable aspects of the human condition is that there is always someone, somewhere, ready to take on the job of worrying about you. It's unavoidable. What *can* be avoided, though, is any unnecessary prolongation of your worrier's attention.

Sarcastic surprise often works:

> *Damn, I* KNEW *there was something I'd forgotten.*

So does bluntness:

> *I thought I'd leave that to you.*

Maybe you find the consequences a bargain at the price:

> *Yes, but I know from experience that penicillin will cure it.*

Or you have chosen to postpone any such consideration:

> *No, that comes next.*

Or you would prefer to avoid such consideration altogether:

> *Of course not. That would take all the fun out of it.*

Or you have hedged your bets with delightfully inverted logic:

> *Only insofar as they will affect the outcome.*

WAS IT GOOD FOR YOU?

Consumer surveys are tiresome at the best of times; when conducted postcoitally they are indecent. Anyone who expects to be graded after sex deserves to be flung out of bed. But assuming that you don't have the energy required for that kind of solution, you can achieve much the same result with a couple of questions of your own:

> *Was* WHAT *good for me?*
>
> *Does that mean it's over?*

Or you can pass comparatively favorable judgment:

> *Better than I expected.*

Or favorable judgment based on a process of elimination:

> *Of course. Who else could it be good for?*

Or you can think about it, and think about it, and think about it, until your companion is unable to resist the urge to repeat, or underline, the question. At which point you call time out:

> *Be patient. I'm trying to remember.*

IS YOUR WORK MORE IMPORTANT THAN OUR RELATIONSHIP?

One of the more pitiable of the apples-and-oranges questions. If you want to focus on its foolishness, you can always go for a playfully self-sabotaging answer:

> *Could you put that in a memo?*

> *That's a fascinating question. I'd like to try that one on the computer.*

Or you might indicate that different people would have different views on the subject:

> *To my boss, it is.*

Or you could put the matter in its proper perspective:

> *No, but it pays better.*

Or you can return the apples and oranges, scrambled:

> *Our relationship* is *my work. I go to the office for fun.*

CAN'T WE STAY FRIENDS?

Apart from being witless in its own right, this grim little query usually comes in the wake of some kind of sickening revelation: Your lover is leaving you for someone else, your wife wants to marry her analyst, your husband wants to marry *his* analyst, your business partner has been forging your name on checks, that sort of thing. But this doesn't mean that you should dismiss the question out of hand.

For one thing, the question doesn't specify with *whom* you might stay friends. Thus:

> *Of course. I intend to stay friends with lots of people.*

Or you can give the conditions under which you two could stay friends:

> *It depends on how versatile you are.*
>
> *Sure, provided we* MAKE *friends first.*

Or you can give the reasons why you think you might be able to stay friends:

> *We probably can. Look how long we've stayed enemies.*
>
> *Why not? We need a change.*

Or you can give an alternative to staying friends:

> *I think I'd be happier if we stayed contemporaries instead.*

All the same, you would be well-advised to clear up a possible misunderstanding:

You're STAYING?

WHAT DO YOU THINK? YOU HAVEN'T SAID ANYTHING ALL EVENING!

One of the great mysteries of the universe is why someone who's determined to bore you to death cannot let you suffer in silence. It's as if people have to hear the agony in your voice before they are convinced that they have wrecked your evening. So perhaps the most economical way of satisfying someone on this score is to let out a bloodcurdling scream and then fall over in a dead faint.

A less histrionic way, but almost as effective, is to alert him to the prospect of a very bumpy conversational road ahead. In a thick accent:

I am with English having trouble please.

Or you may retreat behind a glazed, faraway visage:

I'm marching to the beat of a different drum, man.

Or you could hint that this line of questioning is not going to be very rewarding:

Do you think there might be a good reason for that?

Or you might try to close the gap between the question and the statement:

Do you want me to think or talk?

Or you may want to correct a misperception:

I have, but under my breath.

HAVE YOU EVER HAD A HOMOSEXUAL AFFAIR?

Assuming that you are not being interviewed by your biographer, you have just been asked a question of stupefying impertinence. How do you deal with it?

With befuddlement:

What's a homosexual?

With *sophisticated* befuddlement:

Is that a question or a proposition?

With sophisticated curiosity:

Why do you want to know, sweetie?

With an offer:

Hold me close and I'll tell you.

With prurient interest:

No, what's it like?

Or, finally, with haughty nonsense:

> *No, I have my affairs catered.*

WHY DON'T YOU MOVE IN WITH HIM?

As you are no doubt all too aware, the world is teeming with free-lance motivational researchers who are eager to hear you account for the way you organize your life. And this question is one of their favorites.

A simple method of deflecting it is to respond with upside-down reasoning:

> *Then I wouldn't be at home when the telephone rings.*

Or to stage a parade of non sequiturs, beginning with:

> *The same reason* YOU *don't.*

This, of course, will elicit an enquiry as to what that reason could be, whereupon you confess that you don't know. And the reason you don't know is that you wouldn't dream of asking such a question yourself.

But if you want to be gentler about it, you can always cite irreconcilable differences:

> *He won't let me bring my killer bees.*

Or confide a dark secret:

> *It wouldn't be so dirty that way.*

Or, better still, betray one of *his* dark secrets:

> *If I did, he would wear my bras* ALL *the time.*

> *He and his grandmother are always fighting.*

> *The leprosy. It shouldn't put me off, but it does.*

HOW COME I'VE NEVER HEARD OF YOU?

How come people think you can explain *their* problems? Anyway, if you're feeling generous, you can take the blame for your questioner's handicap:

> *Because I move in mysterious ways.*

Or you can shift it on to a third party:

> *Because my PR guy has a bad stammer.*

Or you can request more information:

> *I can't answer that until I know whom you* HAVE *heard of.*

Or you may care to speculate on the state of the person's general knowledge:

> *Because I wasn't named Christ, Hitler, or Farrah Fawcett.*

I've never been on "Hollywood Squares."

Or you might want to take this opportunity to deliver some bad news:

Because I asked your wife to be discreet about it.

DO YOU STILL LOVE ME?

And now, from those wonderful folks who brought you "Have You Stopped Beating Your Wife?" comes this tender and heartwarming sequel. Beware. A question can be stupid and still be loaded.

You can disarm it with deliberate ambiguity:

As much as I ever did.

Or, less ambiguously:

STILL? *You believed all that stuff I told you?*

With strings attached:

That depends. What did you do for me today?

With implied criticism attached:

Whenever you're not too tired.

Jokingly:

Don't get personal.

Jokingly but wickedly:

> *You know, you're the third person who's asked me that today.*

HOW CAN YOU SAY THAT?

Makes you wonder, doesn't it? It seemed so easy when you said it. And now you're being asked to provide an instant analysis.

All right, but first you might want to check out the taste of your audience:

> *How would you* LIKE *me to say it?*

Or its stamina:

> *Over and over again.*

Don't be shy about indicating your emotional range:

> *Once more, with feeling.*

Or your educational range:

> *Oh, in French, German, Italian. What's your favorite?*

At the same time you ought to specify the limits of your patience:

> *Listen carefully, because I don't want to have to say it a third time.*

But if you've already reached the limits of
your patience, there's a handy *quid pro quo:*

> *How can* YOU *say* THAT?

ARE YOU DOING ANYTHING
THURSDAY NIGHT?

Here's an excellent example of the short distance between enticement and entrapment. Enticement is fine,
as in: "If you're free Thursday night, we'd like you to
join us for. . . ." That way it's left to you to decide just
how enticing the proposition is. But when it's phrased
as above, you are (quite deliberately) given no clue as
to what you might be letting yourself in for.

This illustrates another truism: You don't
have to be a fool to ask a stupid question.

Likewise, you're no fool if you give a stupid
answer:

> *Thursday night?* BINGO NIGHT?

Or a precisely vague answer:

> *I never do just anything—even on Thursday
> night.*

Or a vaguely comprehensive answer:

> *Nothing illegal.*

Or a comprehensively discouraging answer:

> *Only until the end of the year. The first*
> *Thursday in January looks good.*

To take a different tack, you can leave the door slightly, suggestively, ajar:

> *Sure. But not* ALL *night.*

Or challengingly open:

> *Make me an offer.*

HOW COME A PRETTY GIRL LIKE YOU ISN'T MARRIED?

When making a statement, a generalization serves to turn an observation into a theory. When making an enquiry, it only serves to guarantee that the question will be a stupid one.

This is a case in point. You haven't been asked why you aren't married; you've been asked why someone *like* you isn't married.

There's only one rational answer:

> *I don't know. I guess you'll have to find*
> *a pretty girl like me and ask her.*

But why be rational when you can be horrible? Thus:

> *How come an ugly person like you* IS?

And you can still be truthful:

> *I work at it.*

Or, if you prefer, truth *and* hurtful:

> *Because I'm more selective than you are.*

Then, too, there's the sliding scale of sexual preferences to which you can refer. Beginning with:

> *It's my lover's fault. She hates the idea.*

Sliding downward:

> *I'm a transvestite. You won't tell, will you?*

Finally, for those whose understanding is illuminated by commercialism:

> *Because I can make more money doing it on a free-lance basis.*

YOU STILL HERE?

There are stupid questions and there are stupid questions. If it's any consolation, they don't come any stupider than this.

Go, as they say, with the flow:

Not that I know of.

Perhaps adding a touch of doubtfulness:

I'm not sure. Have you got a mirror on you?

Or a touch of schizophrenia:

Partially.

If you care to explain your fate:

Yeah, the guards got me going over the wall.

But there's no need to explain. Be fatalistic. Show that existentialism lives:

I'm afraid so. How about you?

4
Nags

DO YOU REALLY WANT THAT CIGARETTE?

The first thing to remember about people who nag is that they can't help it. They are driven. The person who accuses, threatens, or insults you generally knows perfectly well what he's doing, while the person who nags you is convinced that he is on a mission to save you. Hence the lugubrious refrain: *I'm only doing it for your own good.* No wonder we enjoy jokes about missionaries being eaten.

The point is that you must never assume that you can get rid of a nagger with one sharp thrust. Naggers don't feel pain. Or, rather, they feel it all the time. Pain is an integral part of their condition, so you'd better be prepared for a long siege unless you can deliver your lines with an air of absolute finality (preferably tinged with nuttiness: don't forget that naggers are highly serious people).

One way of handling this question is to build your response around the emphasis on *that* cigarette:

>*Not especially. It was just the first one that came out of the pack.*

>*No, it's the* NEXT *one I really want. This one's just to get me in the mood.*

Another way is to address yourself to the nagger's concern about the level of your desire for the cigarette, how much you *really want* it:

>*No, I'm just breaking it in for a friend.*

>*Only for smoking. Too much fresh air makes me cough.*

Finally, you may be forgiven (though not, of course, by the nagger) for suspecting that the question does not proceed from a sense of public-spiritedness where your health is concerned, but from a sense of private deprivation where the cigarette is concerned:

>*Just be patient. You can have it when I'm finished with it.*

DON'T YOU THINK YOU'VE HAD ENOUGH TO DRINK?

Here we go again. But don't despair. Remember that the only requisite for success at nagging, like jogging, is the ability to keep it up.

So your best bet is to try to undermine the nagger's morale, and therefore his stamina. This can be achieved by taking the pivotal word and using it as the basis for a diversionary tactic:

Enough for what?

Or as the basis for an unexpected roadblock:

Enough for YOU, *maybe. Not enough for me.*

Then again, it's often possible to smother a question by embracing the assumptions that led up to it:

I'm far too drunk to answer a question like that.

Squeezing tighter, while tickling:

How kind. Just a little one, please.

Ultimately, shock treatment may be called for. In which case try full-frontal exposure to the Awful Truth:

No, I can still hear you.

YOU'RE MAKING A FOOL OF YOURSELF

Mark Twain once said that it takes *two* people to really hurt you: your enemy who slanders you, and your friend who makes sure you hear about it. This is precisely why naggers usually end up frustrated. They're always trying to do two jobs at once.

Here's a good example. Your "friend" is voicing an opinion that even your most dedicated enemies would hesitate to endorse publicly. Thus, you can capitalize on your friend's role-confusion by offering an immediate endorsement of your own, coupled with a gratuitous admission that reverses the direction of the whole complaint:

> *I know, I'm always the last one to get on the bandwagon.*

On the other hand, you may endorse the observation in the metallic tones of a quizmaster, and at the same time distance yourself both literally and metaphorically:

> *Okay, you got that one right. Ready for the next one? What am I doing now?*

What you are doing, of course, is walking away. But wait. You've left untouched a number of rich ambiguities in the nag. For instance, there's nothing wrong with making something—anything—of yourself so long as you're not stealing somebody's act:

> *Did you think you had exclusive rights on the part?*

Nor should you be criticized for expending your talents on yourself:

> *Well, it's more of a challenge than making a fool of YOU.*

And in any case you can always claim that you were only moonlighting as a fool:

> *Actually, I was just killing time until you came along and gave me a chance to make a real bastard of myself.*

IF YOU DON'T MIND MY SAYING SO . . .

You will have to move quickly if you want to trip up the nagger who lurches into your consciousness with: "If you don't mind my saying so. . . ." But it's worth the effort. Even if it doesn't stop him, it forces him into the position of a self-conscious bull who suddenly realizes that he has been lured into a china shop.

You can do it playfully:

> *Wait. You're not going to talk dirty, are you?*

Or more harshly:

> *Does ANYBODY mind what you say?*

Or you can dissociate yourself from the proceedings:

> *Go right ahead. I'll be back in half an hour.*

Or you can wave him on, with a warning flag:

> *I almost certainly will, but do continue.*

Or you can check on his preparedness to continue:

> *Just in case I do, what's your contingency plan?*

But since it's not always possible to stop a nagger at full gallop, you should keep a line in reserve:

> *Well, since I DID mind, how do you propose to make it up to me?*

YOU EAT LIKE A BIRD

The ghost of the Jewish Mother strikes again. You can strike back by agreeing cordially, with amplification:

> *You're right. I DON'T talk with food in my mouth.*

Or with precision:

> *A buzzard, to be exact.*

Or with justification:

> *It's better than eating like a fly.*

Or with justification:

> *No longer. I've gone off worms.*

Otherwise, you can treat the statement as a command resulting from a mix-up in the agenda:

> *I thought it was* YOUR *turn to do the animal impersonations.*

IF ONLY YOU KNEW HOW RIDICULOUS THAT LOOKS

One thing you can say for naggers: They're dependable. As a matter of fact, that's one thing you can say *to* them:

> *I don't need to know. I can always depend on you to tell me.*

Though you may want to solicit further advice:

> *Do you think it would help?*

Or you can mention one of the advantages of ignorance:

> *I'm glad I don't know. I might start sounding like you.*

On the other hand, you might want to put an end to any speculation about if only *you* knew:

> *But only I* DO *know. That's why it's always successful.*

Similarly, the converse raises an interesting point:

> *If I were the only one who knew, what would you be talking about now?*

I SUPPOSE YOU'RE SULKING NOW

Before you are tempted to think that suicide offers the only escape from the determined nagger, remember that the whole point of nagging is to keep it up. If a nagger lets you retreat into silent contemplation of your sufferings, he will be deprived of the whole reason for his miserable existence. Nevertheless, it's always worth trying a sudden plunge into silence. With any luck, the nagger won't dive in after you.

But if he does, you can encourage him to scramble out again:

> *Don't change the subject. I was just getting interested.*

Or you can reward his tenacity by calling attention to it:

> *I see. And what's that* YOU'RE *doing?*

Or you can give him the courage to go on (and on):

> *Please, don't let* THAT *stop you.*

Or you can help him to see the error of his ways:

> *No, thinking. There's a subtle difference,*
> *you know.*

Or you may feel called upon to explain the
timing of your leap out of the conversation:

> *Now seems as good a time as any.*

DO YOU KNOW WHAT THAT DOES
TO YOUR BODY?

This is another one of those Awful Warnings disguised
as a Concerned Query. Needless to say, you will ignore the warning and play along with the disguise.

In a quietly boastful manner, perhaps:

> *Of course I do. You realize I'm*
> *ninety-six.*

Or with the enthusiasm of the born-again
satyr:

> *Boy, do I! Drives 'em crazy, doesn't it?*

Or you might simply explain that there's a
sort of poetic justice involved:

> *Nothing compared to what my body does*
> *to IT. Ever looked inside a septic tank?*

Or express reciprocal concern:

> *Do you know what questions like that do*
> *to your mind?*

Lastly, if whatever it is you're doing is clearly detrimental to the appearance and well-being of your body, you can always be philosophical about it:

> *Yes, gives me a scapegoat. What do you blame* YOUR *body on?*

I JUST HATE TO SEE YOU RUINING YOUR HEALTH

In the first place, this kind of announcement is bound to make you wonder:

> *Why do you watch?*

Considering that you are familiar with the sensation:

> *Me too. That's why I don't look.*

Then again, it may be your fitness for the task that has occasioned such distress:

> *Why? Do you know somebody who could do a better job?*

Or your neglect of more suitable victims:

> *Whose would you like me to ruin?*

Or your choice of your health as something to ruin:

> *It's better than ruining my clothes.*

In any case, you know the feeling:

>*Not as much as I hate to see* YOU *ruining it.*

I HOPE YOU'VE FINALLY LEARNED YOUR LESSON

The lesson is, of course, that certain people are to be avoided whenever possible. At the same time, people who hope that you've learned your lesson do afford a splendid opportunity for you to teach a thing or two of your own.

You can, first of all, treat the line as a plain expression of a hope:

>*That's your first wish. You have two more.*

Or as a reference to the advanced hour:

>*Why? Is it getting late?*

Or as a valediction:

>*Finally? You mean that's the end of it?*

Or as a chance for you to report on your progress:

>*I've started working on it. I gave up trying to learn* YOUR *lesson.*

Or as an occasion for you to marvel at that progress:

>*Isn't the human mind wonderful?*

THAT'S A DISGUSTING HABIT

Like all verdicts rendered without the use of a personal pronoun, this one leaves the question of the speaker's attitude open. The sentence, after all, could be an unsolicited testimonial:

I KNEW *you'd like it.*

Or an observation that needs qualifying:

Only when someone is watching.

Or one that provides illumination:

That probably accounts for its popularity.

Or one that invites concurrence and comparison:

I know. Like nagging.

But, alas, it's probably meant as a notice that your taste needs improving, and thus it places on you the responsibility for discovering how comprehensively you need to modify your behavior:

So is oral sex. Want me to give that up, too?

DON'T BE SUCH A STICK-IN-THE-MUD

In such company, it's no wonder that you haven't tried to be the life of the party. But here's your chance to liven things up a bit.

For a start, you might want to congratulate your friendly adviser on the perceptiveness underlying his suggestion:

> *At least you have a shrewd understanding of the present environment.*

Although this does raise a question:

> *Is there something* BETTER *to be in mud?*

You can also admit to your discomfort:

> *Believe me, I would rather be a stick in something else.*

While making it clear that you are not insulting anybody:

> *How can you refer to these nice people as mud?*

Or perhaps you were wrong not to pay closer attention to that word *such:*

> *What kind of a stick-in-the-mud would you like me to be?*

STOP REPEATING YOURSELF

Of course, if you *have* been repeating yourself, it could be because you deemed it necessary in the light of the other person's attention span. But it's not a good idea to say that. The last thing you want to do is to convert a nagger into an accuser. You want to convert him or her into a ghost.

You might begin by showing some uncertainty as to what kind of reproduction he has in mind.

> *Are you working for Planned Parenthood now?*
>
> *I have. That's what the vasectomy was for.*

Or doubt about what your friend wants to hear:

> *Whom should I repeat?*

Or concern about fidelity to the original:

> *I would, but I can't trust anybody else to repeat me accurately.*

Or concern about your friend's sensibilities:

> *Which word was it that bothered you?*

Or you can always initiate a dance that ends with a deal:

> *What? . . . What? . . . Okay, I will if you will.*

I TOLD YOU SO

This should be the title of the last cut on the album of *The Naggers' Greatest Hits*. For no one who is really dedicated to nagging is ever satisfied with simply telling you what you should or should not do; the true nagger waits for you to suffer some setback as a result of ignoring his advice, whereupon he is driven to tell you that he "told you so."

This immediately gives you the framework for a reply:

> *And now you've told me that you told me. Want to go for the hat trick?*

Or you can acknowledge the wisdom of the advice, at the same time suggesting that it was misdirected:

> *That's the problem. You should have told somebody who listens to you.*

Or you can admit that you underestimated the counsel because of your experience with the counsellor:

> *That's why I went ahead. You should warn me when you're about to say something intelligent.*

Or you can blame the unreliability of the oral tradition:

> *You should have put it in writing.*

Or you can pay homage to the sagacity of
those wiser than you:

> *No wonder people line up to get your advice.*

YOU ASKED FOR IT!

Sung to the same tune as "I Told You So," this
wretched line exposes the longing for retribution that
lurks in the hearts of all naggers. Nevertheless, there
are ways to get them to change their tune.

One of them goes something like this:

> *I did? Recently?*

Or like this:

> *Not specifically. Not for* THAT *anyway.*

A variation on this theme goes:

> *I only asked for part of it. The rest was
> ad lib.*

A slipperier variation:

> *No, I asked for corned beef on rye. It's a
> common mistake.*

But you can still acknowledge "it" with
graciousness:

> *I must have asked nicely. I certainly got
> it.*

Even with measured delight:

> *Well, it's good to know you can still get same-day service.*

DO YOU INTEND TO GO OUT LOOKING LIKE THAT?

Look at it this way: An evening that begins like this at least isn't going to be a disappointment. In fact, it could even be a giggle—especially if you like to see people dig their own graves. Offer a shovel:

> *Do you intend to go out talking like that?*

Of course, it's always possible—not probable, but possible—that the seemingly contemptuous reference was to your youthful appearance:

> *It would be nice. But, alas, I'll probably have aged by then.*

Or, then again, to your prematurely weary appearance:

> *No, I'm sure I'll cheer up when I get out of here.*

You might even express cautious optimism:

> *To begin with. Who knows what will happen after that?*

In any event:

> *As long as* YOU'RE *with me, no one will notice.*

And there's your at-home image to consider:

> *I certainly wouldn't* STAY IN *looking like this.*

COME ON, SMILE!

Being ordered to smile is like seeing the LAUGH sign go on at a performance of *The Diary of Anne Frank,* but worse.

You can respond with an equally difficult-to-fulfill-on-the-spot order:

> *Come on, die!*

Or you can ask for an explanation of the order:

> *About what?*

Or you can guess at the explanation:

> *Why? You're leaving?*

Or you can comply conditionally:

> *Okay. But do you mind if I do it somewhere else?*

Perhaps you want a test drive before making a commitment:

> *Can you show me how? . . . Oh, if that's what it looks like I think I'd rather not.*

Better still, *get* a commitment:

> *All right, if you promise not to look.*

YOU DO THAT JUST TO UPSET ME

If this is true, you ought to be exultant:

> *It's* WORKING?!

And even if it's only half-true, a glimpse of your motivation can be rewarding:

> *Not altogether. But that's certainly part of it.*

Be specific if you like:

> *I also do it to make you angry.*

Or be testing, severely testing:

> *What makes you think so, flyface?*

After all, consider that naggers exist to be demoralized:

> *Can you think of a better reason?*

WELL, IF IT MAKES YOU HAPPY . . .

Nags never end with a bang, always with a whimper. As often as not, the whimpering has to do with your happiness—which is hardly surprising when you remember that the nagger's deepest, darkest fear is that you aren't suffering as much as he is.

You might hint at this by finishing the sentence for him:

> *I know: If it makes me happy you'll hang yourself.*

Or you might want to point out one of the sad facts of life when there's a nagger around:

> *If it makes me happy, it will be a new experience.*

Another and particularly poignant way to fill in the blank is with the promise of more pain to come:

> *If it does, you'll be the first to know.*

Should you want to make it confession time:

> *It does. I loved "The Texas Chain Saw Massacre," too.*

A different sort of confession:

> *Who wants to be happy? I just want to be rich.*

But, with naggers, sometimes you have to be cruel to be kind:

> *It doesn't matter as long as it makes you miserable.*

5
Teases, Bores, Grumps, and Other Pests

HI! REMEMBER ME?

You've been spotted. But don't panic. You can still get away. Respond calmly, matter-of-factly:

> *Not from the front.*

Or you can make a little extra effort:

> *Hard to say. Do you have any old pictures of yourself?*

> *The* GREETING *is certainly familiar.*

Perhaps it's something they *did* that's supposed to be memorable:

> *For what?*

You might as well take a guess:

> *Bankruptcy court, 1958, wasn't it?*

Or even a gamble:

> *I thought I told you I didn't want any encyclopedias.*

Ultimately, you may just have to give it to them straight:

> *Not unless I have to.*

GETTING A LITTLE THIN ON TOP, I SEE

Some observers of the human condition are valuable assets to society. Some are not. This one is a definite liability. You can cut your losses, though, by explaining (with exaggerated emphasis, if the person happens to be overweight):

> *A diet has to start somewhere.*

And you can give credit where credit is due:

> *Hair Watchers has made all the difference.*

Or you can maintain that you parted with your hair as an act of charity rather than of vanity:

> *Yes, I gave at the office.*

Or perhaps it was a sacrifice made on behalf of a higher cause:

> *That's the one thing I don't like about sex: too much of it makes your hair fall out.*

You're entitled, too, to a matching observation:

> *And you're still a bit thick on top.*

YOU'RE REALLY DRESSED TO KILL TONIGHT

A little old-fashioned, this tease, even rather sweet. Alas, however, people who have a sweet, old-fashioned way of teasing can be as big a pain as their more waspish counterparts. So you should have an effective painkiller handy.

One is the slowly dawning discovery:

That wasn't the original idea, but I must say it does have a certain appeal.

Another is the genial agreement, with explanation:

I know. I got tired of dressing to wound.

Or less genial agreement, with contrast:

That's my style—unlike yours, which is to bore people to death.

Then there is mild alarm:

The shoulder holster is THAT obvious?

And mild suggestiveness:

Actually, I was planning to kill most of tonight UNdressed.

WELL, IF YOU ASK ME . . .

And of course nobody ever does. It's not only unnecessary, it's unrewarding:

> *I may be crazy, but I'm not that crazy.*

But before you walk away, it might be worthwhile to find out how dismal the prospect would be if you stayed:

> *And if I* DON'T? *Will you still tell me?*

Or you can try to find out if others have been faced with the same prospect:

> *Has anyone ever done that? Ask you?*

Or you can give some solace even as you depart:

> *I won't, but I'll go and find somebody who will.*

However, should you fail to get away in time to avoid hearing the wretched opinion foreshadowed above, you can at least do something about avoiding the *next* opinion:

> *Now we know why nobody asked you.*

GOOD WEATHER FOR DUCKS!

Part-time meteorologists, like full-time locusts, have been known to cause plagues for which there is no known cure. But that doesn't mean they can't be persuaded to infest someone else's territory. In this instance, you might begin by accepting their assessment, but with a rider attached:

> *Yes, but it's death for conversation.*

Or you can question the relevance of the assessment:

> *Who cares about ducks?*

Or question the authority for making it:

> *What makes you so sure?*

Or try to determine its origins:

> *You talk to* DUCKS?

Or you may choose to stress its limited applicability:

> *Maybe for* YOUR *ducks. Mine hate it.*

Or you can dismiss it altogether:

> *Are you kidding? It's raining!*

HOW DO YOU EXPECT ME TO DO TWO THINGS AT ONCE?

Here's your chance to be honest:

> *Clumsily.*

Even brutally honest:

> *I don't. I just get a kick out of watching you try.*

> *Because I have faith in miracles.*

Or resigned:

> *With your usual flair.*

Or optimistic:

> *Better than you've BEEN doing them.*

Or realistic:

> *With practice.*

Or patient:

> *You don't have to do them AT ONCE. I'm not in a hurry.*

NOT TONIGHT, I HAVE A HEADACHE

Enough said. That's the trouble. It's *always* enough said. Worse, it always will be, unless *you* say something.

Perhaps something cheerful:

> *Then I have good news for you. It's not your head that I want tonight.*

Or you can supply a somewhat unflattering diagnosis:

> *It's probably only a pulled muscle.*

Indeed, a prescription might be in order:

> *Don't think about sex and it'll go away.*

Or you can proceed, acknowledging your one consolation:

> *At least I won't be spoiling anything for you.*

YOU'RE BEING JUDGMENTAL

This is one of those blessed lines which come with a perfect, built-in reply:

> *Is there something wrong with being judgmental?*

Think about that one for a moment. How do you answer it without being judgmental?

Among the other satisfying replies, you might try a couple of less subtle variations on the first one:

> *You're right . . . in my judgment, that is.*

> *But of course. Is it possible* NOT *to be?*

Or you can divulge your reasons for being judgmental:

> *I certainly hope so. I'd hate to be sent to one of those institutions for people who* CAN'T *make judgments.*

Or you may care to make a fine distinction:

> *No, just opinionated.*

Or you may want to divulge the benefits of being judgmental:

> *That's what gives me my great moral and intellectual superiority.*

There remains the possibility that you have excited jealousy by stealing the scene with your judgments:

> *We can change roles if you like. I'll be stupid and* YOU *be judgmental.*

I JUST LOVE YOUR HAIR THAT COLOR

This is a truly wicked remark, especially if it is made in the presence of others. Happily, it is also one that can be turned aside with relative ease. To begin with, as the color of someone's hair is an unusual thing to love, and exceedingly unusual as the object of a public declaration of affection, you might want to establish the basis of the initial attraction:

Why? Does it look funny or something?

Or at least gauge the depth of the devotion:

How much?

If you're still not sure about the sincerity of the compliment, you can accept it provisionally on behalf of your hair:

It will be pleased to hear that, I'm sure.

Or you can acknowledge it graciously:

Yes, I find it brings out the tact in people.

Or even hold out the possibility of requited love:

Maybe I'll give you a lock of it.

But people who proclaim love for your hair color will probably be happy just to know that they are not alone in their strange passion:

*Really? Then I must introduce you to
Mrs. X. She's another one who loves it.
You two will have a lot to talk about.*

DON'T GET CARRIED AWAY!

Cautionary injunctions have a charm all their own.
And a logic all their own, too. To illustrate, you might
reasonably wonder:

What should I get instead?

Or you might reasonably pose the alternative:

It's either that or have to walk away.

Or point out the pointlessness of the warning:

*I can't get carried away today. My
bearers are off.*

Or take a correctional position:

I'm not. I'm just trying to keep awake.

Or give reassurance:

*Don't panic, you'll still be able to find
me.*

I WISH I COULD AFFORD TO SHOP THERE

As wishes go, this one is straightforward enough on the surface. But there's a nasty undertow pulling in the opposite direction: ". . . and since I can't, I wish *you* couldn't either." Never struggle against a dangerous current. Go with it:

> *I do, too.*

But remember that people who say this have a problem. Try to get to the bottom of it:

> *Why? Have they been rude to you at Woolworth's?*

Or try to cheer them up:

> *Oh, I'm sure they have* SOMETHING *you could afford.*

Or persuade them that they're not missing anything:

> *They don't have anything you'd like. It's all quality stuff.*

Or do them a favor by showing them how they *could* afford to shop there:

> *You could if you got rid of your shrink. I mean, those sessions aren't doing you any good, are they?*

Or maybe all that's needed is reassurance
that the experience of shopping there won't
be humiliating:

> *I don't think they'd mind, if you dressed
> up a bit and kept your voice down.*

I ADMIRE YOUR OPTIMISM

One should never take admiration lightly, of course,
but this does not apply to the person who professes
admiration sarcastically. He can be taken very lightly
indeed. You might begin with a display of self-
appreciation:

> *It* is *admirable, isn't it?*

> *I'm rather proud of it myself.*

Adding, perhaps:

> *That's why I cultivate it.*

Or if you're greedy for praise, you can try for
a bonus:

> *What about my new shoes? Don't you
> think they're nice, too?*

Or you can accept the praise as evidence of
the person's improving psychological condition:

> *I think that's a healthy sign. Keep it up.*

Or you may simply want to repay the compliment:

> *Yours is quite stunning, too.*

WHAT DO YOU DO?

Not a bad question, really. It only becomes bad when it's asked by someone whose attentions you would like to escape. Then you wriggle out of his clutches by being incomprehensible:

> *Nothing. I'm too busy most of the time.*

Or criminal:

> *Two to ten, if I'm lucky. Depends on whether the victim dies.*

Or boring:

> *I watch TV a lot.*

Or mysterious:

> *I'm not allowed to talk about it. Could get us both into trouble.*

Or depressing:

> *About as well as can be expected.*

Or candid:

> *As little as possible.*

Or weird:

> *I'm a lifeguard in a car wash.*

SO YOU CONSIDER YOURSELF AN EXPERT ON ———, DO YOU?

This dreary question is typically asked by someone who tends to lurk somewhere on the outskirts of a conversation until your ideas on a subject are all out in the open. Then comes this *pop pop* of sniper fire from the bushes. You can run for cover if you like, but it's more fun to return the fire:

> *No, I'm an expert on mental retardation. Whoever sent you must have been pulling your leg.*

You might plead mistaken identity:

> *No, I only* SEEM *like an expert to you.*

Or mistaken humility:

> *No. The fact that I'm a world-famous authority on the subject doesn't necessarily make me an expert.*

Or excruciating humility:

> *I seldom consider myself at all. I'm always considering others.*

Or you might resort to off-handed candor:

> *Only when I don't have anything better to think about.*

> *You know, I haven't the time anymore. It's all I can do just to* BE *an expert.*

DO YOU LIKE CHILDREN?

Ever heard a child ask this question? Of course not. They don't have to ask. Most of them are bright enough to *know* if you like them. It's only dim grown-ups who feel enriched by such information. So give them what they want.

An affirmation, maybe:

> *Of course. I used to go to school with them.*

Though you can be discriminating:

> *Some of them, eventually, late in life.*

And you can specify under what conditions:

> *Only when there are no men/women* (choose one) *available.*

Or you may need clarification:

> *Like them to* WHAT?

If you want to answer more fully and help-fully, you should indicate precisely where children come in the hierarchy of your enthusiasms:

> *They're okay if they're cooked just right. But I still prefer veal.*

But it's probably easiest to reply by sketching in the boundaries of your taste:

> *Not in person.*

GUESS WHAT I PAID FOR THIS!

There are basically—perhaps exclusively—two types of people who derive pleasure from reading their price tags to you: upwardly mobile bargain-hunters and downwardly mobile respectability-hunters. It's a toss-up which is the more boring.

You can always play it safe:

Money.

Or silly:

Buttons? Bottle caps? Food stamps?

Or both safe and silly:

Eight hundred thousand dollars?

If you're dealing with a bargain-hunter, you should be depressing:

About what it's worth.

Or shattering:

Too much.

If it's a respectability-hunter, ditto:

Twenty percent down?

Or ditto, ditto:

Your last few cents, judging by the way you're dressed.

I KNOW YOU WILL HAVE A SECOND HELPING

Granted, it's within the realm of possibility that your eating habits have caused you to take up more air space than those around you might deem proper, but that's no excuse for such unbridled presumptuousness. Now's the time to bare your teeth for real.

Pointedly, pointing:

> *Of* THAT?

Recalling what went before:

> *You think the first one was a helping?*

Declining, still not forgetting what went before:

> *I'm afraid not. Nobody could be* THAT *hungry.*

Panicking, tentatively:

> *Oh, it's come to force-feeding, has it?*

Acquiescing, sympathetically:

> *Yes, I'll have yours. I always go to the aid of dieters.*

Leaving, abruptly:

> *Yes. To go.*

WELL, NO ONE'S PERFECT

It is mildly ironic, but wholly appropriate, that this nugget of revelatory wisdom is always, but *always,* revealed by someone whose imperfections are so lavish in scale as to make even God cringe.

But leave the cringing to God. In this situation, a straight face is more effective:

> *True. I wonder why that is.*

Perhaps a straight face flushed with new-found knowledge:

> *Ah, that explains everything.*

Or with frustration:

> NOW *he tells me.*

With disappointment, shading into grief:

> *Another illusion shattered.*

With disgust, shading into theology:

> *Are you calling Jesus a liar?*

With forgiveness, and a soft hint of Messianism:

> *I'm afraid . . . you've been . . . misinformed.*

And be sure to smile angelically when you say it.

WHAT NUMBER IS THIS?

It is axiomatic that, just as a watched fire never lights, a listened-for telephone never rings. As far as the fire is concerned, this constitutes the Bad News; the Good News is that the fire will light sooner or later regardless of how much you fret over it. But with the telephone the bad news simply turns into worse news: Sure, the phone will ring—you can bet on it—but it will ring (you can bet on this, too) just after you have stepped into the shower, or sat down to eat, or climbed into bed.

Worse still, there is the possibility that when you answer it the voice on the other end will not belong to anyone you were hoping to hear from—or indeed to anyone you know. It will be some stuttering half-wit who wants to know what number he has called.

Tell him the truth:

> *The wrong one.*

At greater length:

> *The one you dialed instead of the one you* SHOULD *have dialed.*

Or, just for fun, you might want to compound his confusion:

> *411. Can I help you?*

But perhaps he's referring to his *own* number:

> *How many guesses do I get?*

Or referring to *you* rather than to your telephone:

> *Actually, we go by names here.*

However, in view of the fact that stupidity, like misery, loves company, perhaps he just wants reassurance that he is not alone in being unable to master the complexities of using a telephone:

> *This makes number two today. So you're not the only one. Keep trying.*

WHY DON'T YOU DO IT YOURSELF?

By now, you have probably realized that when you are handed a grumpy line with a question mark attached to it, it is like receiving a gift certificate. You can choose how you want to cash it in.

Flatteringly:

> *You do it so much better.*

Sarcastically:

> *Because I'd miss the stimulating conversation.*

Mysteriously:

> *I'm superstitious.*

Hippily:

> *Because I think it's important to share experiences.*

Philosophically, demonstrating once and for all your special flair for seeing the Big Picture:

> *If God had meant me to do it myself, He wouldn't have put* YOU *here.*

When All
Else Fails:

The
Bottom Lines

While, generally speaking, you should always try to tailor your lines to fit the individual remarks that provoke you, there will inevitably be times when you find it difficult, if not impossible, to come up with a line on the spot that you feel is adequate to deal with the provocation. You should therefore be prepared for these situations by having at the ready a few all-purpose all-weather comebacks. Such as:

Isn't everyone?

This line is particularly effective in countering accusations like "You're lying!" or "You're making a fool of yourself," as well as for squelching snide questions like "All alone tonight?" or "Still looking for a job?" And of course its twin—*Doesn't everyone?*—is similarly effective where the grammar shifts but the intent doesn't: "You think you're so clever" or "Do you really want that cigarette?"

When confronted with truly stupid, boring questions—"Do you like children?" . . . "Do you believe in God?" . . . "What do you think of Jackie Onassis?"—you could do worse than to dust off that old standby:

Compared to what?

With more aggressive questions—"What are you rebelling against?" . . . "What do you want from me?" . . . "What's in it for you?"—there is always the immortal Brando line:

What have you got?

Also worth keeping in your arsenal is a line that will put out almost any fire started by the personal pronoun *I:* "I wouldn't do that if I were you" . . . "I didn't appreciate that!" . . . "I don't like your attitude" . . . "I have a headache tonight" . . . "I don't care what you think" . . . and so forth. The line is based on the assumption that the other person's attention span is measurable in microseconds. Thus, after a short pause:

How about NOW?

There's an equally silly-but-effective line for dousing inflammatory statements beginning with *You* ("You don't know what you're talking about" . . . "You should think before you speak" . . . "You're not going to get away with that" . . . "You must be joking"). It is a line that was once used with devastating comic effect by W. C. Fields, and for best results should be employed with something approaching The Master's air of slightly distracted martyrdom:

My error.

Just as every baseball team keeps one or two utility infielders in reserve, men who can play any of a number of positions reasonably well, so should you have on hand a couple of lines that can be sent in to plug sudden gaps in your defense. For unpleasant or asinine remarks rendered as statements, I would suggest:

Whatever you say.

The line may seem lackluster at first glance, but it is remarkably versatile. If you flip back through the book I think you will be surprised at how few lines there are which can't be handled by this one.

Likewise, most of the nasty insinuations that come at you in the form of questions can be fielded with:

I give up. Why?

(Or, of course, depending on the question: *I give up. How? Who? What? When?* etc.)

My personal favorite for dealing with awkward questions—especially angry, rambling, accusatory questions—is the line John Mitchell made famous, or infamous, in his stone-faced testimony before the Senate Watergate committee:

Could you repeat the question?

This line can work wonders for you. In the first place, it dares your questioner to look foolish, because *any* question repeated verbatim begins to sound a little silly the second time around. Furthermore, it still leaves you with the option of using one of the other lines above, or of asking for yet another repetition—thereby challenging your questioner not just to look foolish but positively ridiculous.

Another excellent way of handling an offensive or disturbing line is to treat it as precisely what it is: a line. Thus, when somebody delivers a line that you would prefer not to respond to directly, you can simply stand there and admire it:

> *Good. Very good. I must remember that one.*

A variation on this technique is to address yourself to the condition of the person who delivered the line:

> *Feeling better now?*

And, lastly, there is what George Bernard Shaw, one of the world's greatest put-down artists, called "the perfect expression of scorn":

> "   !"

Silence. Absolute, sepulchral, wall-to-wall silence. It never fails.

Perfect English?
Perfect English?
Perfect English??

Communicating is easy
once you have the proper tools.

Develop your speech, vocabulary,
spelling, writing with these excellent language
skills titles from Pocket Books.

_____ 44657	COMPLETE LETTER WRITER	$2.95
_____ 82464	ENGLISH VERBAL IDIOMS, F.T. Wood	$2.50
_____ 83230	FASTER READING SELF-TAUGHT, Harry Shefter	$2.95
_____ 83486	A GUIDE TO BETTER COMPOSITIONS, Harry Shefter	$2.50
_____ 82759	HOW TO PREPARE TALKS AND ORAL REPORTS, Harry Shefter	$2.25
_____ 42415	INSTANT VOCABULARY, Ida Ehrlich	$2.95
_____ 43662	MERRIAM-WEBSTER DICTIONARY	$2.75
_____ 43664	MERRIAM-WEBSTER THESAURAS	$2.95

?????

_____43883 QUESTIONS YOU ALWAYS WANTED TO ASK
ABOUT ENGLISH But Were Afraid to Raise
Your Hand, Maxwell Nurnberg $2.50

_____43572 THE QUICK AND EASY WAY TO EFFECTIVE
SPEAKING $2.75

_____44739 SHORT CUTS TO EFFECTIVE ENGLISH,
Harry Shefter $2.95

_____43140 6 MINUTES A DAY TO PERFECT SPELLING,
Harry Shefter $2.50

_____44837 6 WEEKS TO WORDS OF POWER, Wilfred Funk $2.75

_____43676 30 DAYS TO A MORE POWERFUL VOCABULARY $2.75

_____42286 WORDS MOST OFTEN MISSPELLED AND
MISPRONOUNCED, Gleeson & Colvin $2.50

INFORMATION IS POWER

With these almanacs, compendiums, encyclopedias, and dictionaries at your fingertips, you'll always be in the know.
Pocket Books has a complete list of essential reference volumes.